Burn Without Burning Out

Other Books by Denise Pyles

Around the Kitchen Table
A Glowing Ember of Courage
It's Just a Little Rain

Free Resources

There are many free resources on practicing micro-mindfulness available on Denise's website. To get instant access, please visit www.denisepyles.com.

Burn Without Burning Out

7 Micro-Mindfulness Habits for Clear Thinking, Decisive Action, and Recovery from Burnout

DENISE PYLES

Burn Without Burning Out.

Copyright ©2024 Denise Pyles.

ISBN: 978-0-9843474-3-8

All rights reserved. No part of this book may be reproduced or transmitted in any form or by any means without written permission from the author.

The author and publisher do not guarantee the results of the information in this book. The author shares educational and informational resources to help you learn mindfulness practice. Your ultimate success or failure will depend on your efforts, particular situations, and innumerable circumstances beyond the author and publisher's knowledge and control.

Published by Denise Pyles | www.denisepyles.com
Chapter illustrations by Elymar Apao | ellymar.org
Cover design by Magrit Baurecht | www.corecreativeteam.com

For Mary

Life keeps nudging me with this question:

As an ordinary person, how will you spend your everyday life doing extraordinary, meaningful work with the time you have left?

—Denise Pyles

Contents

CHAPTER 1	From Nun to Big Tech Program Manager	1
CHAPTER 2	Forming Mindful Habits	13
CHAPTER 3	Find Your True North	27
	Habit #1 – Focus on the Essential	29
CHAPTER 4	Clear the Chaos	41
	Habit #2 – Set Your Intention	43
	Habit #3 – Make the Most of Your Time	61
CHAPTER 5	Mind the Moment	83
	Habit #4 – Practice the Pause	85
CHAPTER 6	Listen to Frogs Before Eating Them	95
	Habit #5 – Give Grace	99
CHAPTER 7	Burn Without Burning Out	113
	Habit #6 – Carry a Symbol of Meaning	115
	Habit #7 – Exercise Gratitude	129
Wrap Up		145
Summary of Chapter Insights		149

Summary of Journal Prompts	157
Bonus Reflection – 10 Essentials for Mindfulness at Work	161
Acknowledgments	169
Notes	171
About the Author	181
Want to Learn More?	183

Chapter 1

From Nun to Big Tech Program Manager

We spend far too much time at work for it not to have deeper meaning.

— Satya Nadella, CEO, Microsoft

A CAREER PIVOT AT MIDLIFE

I'm a former nun working at Microsoft.

For those who may not be familiar with the term, a "nun" means a "religious sister," a woman who professes religious vows and lives in a community with other women.

I was a Roman Catholic nun for eight years, living with other women in houses known as convents across the United States.

When people think of nuns, they often think of movie

characters, like Whoopi Goldberg in "Sister Act," or famous nuns like Mother Teresa. My experience as a nun was different.

"Did you wear a habit?" is a question most people ask me when they find out I was a nun. My quick response is, "Only bad ones."

All kidding aside, some religious orders still wear a habit, an identifier for nuns. A habit is a unique clothing worn by religious sisters or brothers that distinguishes them as nuns or monks.

The community I belonged to did not wear habits. I dressed in ordinary clothes and wore a cross or religious pin that identified me as a nun.

Two Nuns in Habits – Rome, Italy, 2015

As a nun, I was privileged to journey with people in their most intense moments of life.

I walked with others during illness, dying, or celebrations such as birthdays, weddings, or anniversaries.

I also journeyed with others throughout their ordinary moments while listening, befriending, empowering, and serving. It was a privilege.

A chronic illness was the turning point for my difficult decision to leave religious life.

I needed to stay rooted in one place to care for my health. I also needed to care for my career when I left the community. I pivoted to the corporate environment.

The company I wanted to work for was Microsoft, yet the road to a career change was not easy.

THE PIVOT TO A CORPORATE CAREER

I had a few short-term corporate experiences plus a stringent application process before experiencing success.

Here were my numbers in getting to Microsoft: **44, 1, 9, and 1** – 44 job applications, 1 vendor rotation, 9 interviews, and 1 job offer.

Forty-four applications are a lot for one company. I knew I would succeed or fail with my work effort and strengths. I just needed someone to give me a chance – more on that story about the manager who hired me later in this book.

MINDFULNESS AT WORK

I learned many skills as a nun.

One of the most important ones was the habit of mindfulness. It turns out that this skill would prove particularly useful in the workplace.

This mindfulness skill, which I developed as a nun, helped me manage the high-stress environment of the corporate world.

The mindful habit of setting your intention at the beginning of the day carried over to Microsoft and helped me prioritize my work on the most important tasks or projects.

The mindful habit of focusing on my essential core values, such as being kind or bringing a positive attitude, helped me stay strong and unshaken when the pressures of work to produce results quickly felt overwhelming.

The mindful habit of practicing the pause helped me slow down my racing mind and be fully present in the moment, especially in my work with colleagues.

These mindfulness skills helped me pivot in midlife from a career in church ministry to a successful, award-winning corporate job, and I had no business experience at the beginning. Zero.

These mindfulness skills, curiosity, and a growth mindset were the critical factors that fueled a successful career path.

Reflect for a moment: *What habits help you navigate a successful career?*

THE SCIENCE OF MINDFULNESS

Research studies on employee burnout have shown that eight weeks of mindfulness reduced stress, anxiety, and emotional exhaustion. It also increased self-compassion, relaxation, and sleep quality.

Practicing mindfulness at work can help solve these common workplace problems:

- **Stress management:** You focus on the present moment and accept complex thoughts and emotions without getting overwhelmed.
- **Improved focus and concentration:** You train your mind to stay present and avoid distractions.
- **Enhanced creativity and problem-solving:** You are open to new possibilities and perspectives.
- **Improved communication and collaboration:** You connect with your thoughts and emotions, which can help you communicate and collaborate more effectively with others.
- **Increased emotional intelligence:** You pay attention to your emotions and those of others, which can lead to stronger relationships.

- **Improved decision-making:** You increase positive emotions and decrease negative emotions, which can lead to better decision-making.
- **Improved well-being:** Mindfulness practices have been linked to several positive outcomes for mental and physical health, such as reduced stress, increased feelings of happiness, and sleep quality.
- **Managing burnout:** You have a sense of balance and perspective in the face of job demands, which can help to prevent burnout.
- **Enhanced resilience:** You develop greater self-awareness and self-regulation, which can help you build strength in the face of stress and adversity.
- **Improved overall performance:** Mindfulness practices can enhance your focus, creativity, and emotional intelligence, which can also result in elevated workplace performance.

What has been helpful for you in managing stress or burnout at work?

THE HABITS FOR MINDFULNESS AT WORK

Mindfulness is another name for spiritual growth, a personal development category.

In short, mindfulness is the art of paying attention to

all of life without judgment to discover threads of meaning in the workplace and your everyday life.

Many people think of practicing mindfulness as meditating for long hours at a time. That is one form of mindfulness. There are many other ways to practice this personal growth method.

As a nun, I learned seven habits that helped me and that continue to help me live a reflective, intentional life, especially in my work.

These habits do not require long hours of meditation. They are short activities that you can do practically anywhere and anytime within an active and busy environment.

This book will provide examples of practicing these tiny habits or micro-mindfulness practices that you can do in ten minutes or less throughout your day. Micro-mindfulness is the same as mindfulness, except the duration is different. Think of them as bite-sized pieces of awareness.

Throughout these pages, I will use the terms mindfulness and micro-mindfulness interchangeably.

By practicing consistent mindfulness, time shifts from a feeling of mindless wandering to an experience of timeless presence.

You are not counting the seconds until work is over by the end of the day. Instead, you become lost in the micro-moments, and your work becomes energizing and fulfilling.

The next chapter, Forming Mindful Habits, will focus on workplace mindfulness before diving into each habit.

TRY THIS

Habit Practice – Journal Prompts and Journaling

I've been journaling consistently for more than 40 years.

Journaling is one of the most sustaining go-to tools for personal growth and well-being that I have used consistently throughout my life.

There are many ways to journal, even if you are not a writer.

You can write, draw, speak, make lists, record notes, doodle, or paint your experience – analog or digital.

You can journal in less than ten minutes at a time, and doing this consistently over time will help you discover patterns of insight in your writing.

There are many ways to document your thoughts, and there is no right or wrong way to journal.

Think about how you operate – making lists, writing longhand essays or diary entries, bullet points, or poetry. Do you like to draw, or are you better at processing your thoughts by speaking them aloud?

Journaling can be as simple as:

- One word
- One phrase
- One bullet point
- One sentence
- One paragraph
- One page

Find what works for you.

Mindfulness is about the art of paying attention to all your life experiences to discover threads of meaning in the workplace and throughout your day.

Take a moment to reflect on what mindfulness means to you before journaling your thoughts.

Spend ten minutes or less reflecting and journaling on the following prompts. As the saying goes in AA (Alcoholics Anonymous), *take what you like and leave the rest.*

Each chapter will conclude with an action – a journal prompt to help you engage and practice the specific mindfulness habit.

Journal prompt #1: *The one thing that helps me pay attention and be fully present to what is happening at work is this:*

_____
_____
_____
_____
_____.

FROM NUN TO BIG TECH PROGRAM MANAGER

CHAPTER INSIGHTS

- The mindfulness skills I learned as a nun helped me pivot in midlife from a career in church ministry to a successful, award-winning corporate job. I had zero business experience at the beginning.
- Mindfulness is the art of paying attention to all of life to discover threads of meaning in the workplace and your everyday life.
- Research on employee burnout has shown that several weeks of mindfulness practice can help reduce stress, improve focus, and enhance resilience.
- As a nun, I learned seven habits that helped me and continue to help me live a reflective, intentional life, especially in my work.
- These habits are not long hours of meditation but short activities that you can do practically anywhere and anytime within an active and busy work environment.

Chapter 2

Forming Mindful Habits

Life is amazing. And then it's awful. And then it's amazing again. And in between the amazing and awful, it's ordinary and mundane and routine. Breathe in the amazing, hold on through the awful, and relax and exhale during the ordinary. That's just living a heartbreaking, soul-healing, amazing, awful, ordinary life. And it's breathtakingly beautiful.

—L.R. Knost

Reflect for a moment about your work.
Do any of these experiences resonate with you?

- *You are constantly distracted by your smartphone.*
- *You struggle to manage your workload while main-*

taining quality relationships among family, friends, and colleagues.
- *You experience an inner ache and long for significant connections.*
- *You live a compartmentalized life that creates a disconnect with your whole self.*
- *You feel burned out, stressed, overworked, exhausted, lonely, weary, or afraid of losing control by over-activity.*
- *Your mind is constantly racing, and you lack connection with others.*
- *You struggle with being consistent in your personal growth toward well-being.*

If so, it may be that too much is coming at you in life – too many distractions, pieces of information, activities, and media. It is overwhelming sometimes.

WHEN WORK IS OUT OF SYNC

What happens when your energy at work feels out of sync, and what do you do about it?

This discombobulated experience often results in a lack of meaningful work, a disconnect with coworkers, and burnout.

To generate your energy at work, it is vital to understand your inner source, empowering you to be your best self and to focus on your core values or belief in your higher power (peace, goodness, harmony, kindness, etc.).

Your attention and practice of mindfulness can help you grow toward meaningful work and profound connections among your colleagues and peers.

HOW MINDFULNESS HELPS REALIGN YOUR ENERGY

Mindfulness is the practice of being fully present and engaged at the moment without judgment or distraction.

Many think mindfulness is about sitting and meditating for several hours a day. That technique is one way. Mindfulness is also about paying attention and intentionally engaging in the moment before you.

When you are distracted, your energy may also feel scattered, making it difficult to focus on what's essential in accomplishing your goals.

Practicing mindfulness can help you realign in several ways.

First, mindfulness can help you become more aware of your thoughts and emotions, allowing you to recognize them without becoming overwhelmed or reactive. This awareness can help when you're feeling scattered or distracted and will enable you to return your attention to the present moment.

Second, mindfulness can help you cultivate a sense of calm and centeredness, which can help you feel focused and energized. When you let go of distractions and external pressures, you can become more attuned to your needs and priorities and focus your energy on the things that matter most.

Third, mindfulness can help you develop greater self-awareness and compassion, which can help you feel more connected to yourself and others. By tuning into your thoughts and emotions, you can create a profound empathy and understanding for yourself and those around you. You can realign your energy in a positive and productive way.

When facing distractions or challenges at work, practicing mindfulness can help you realign your energy by allowing you to focus on the present moment, cultivate calm and centeredness, and develop greater self-awareness and compassion.

UNDERSTANDING MINDFULNESS IN YOUR DAY-TO-DAY

During my theological studies, in preparation for being a nun, I took a course on the spirituality of Alcoholics Anonymous (AA).

In this class, I heard one of the best definitions of spirituality that stays with me to this day.

Step 2 of the AA 12-Step Program states, "Came to believe that a Power greater than ourselves could restore us to sanity."

Alcoholics Anonymous defines spirituality as "having all one's energy move in the same direction." This energy is called GOD, meaning "Good Orderly Direction."

AA's definition of spirituality means all your energy is moving in the same direction toward your higher power – how you name this power greater than yourself.

The course widened my perspective on this spiritual energy as mindfulness and the holistic energy of well-being.

So, what does it mean to have all your energy flowing in the same direction?

Much like the experience of love, it's hard to describe, but you know it when you've experienced it. "Energy flowing in the same direction" is the opposite of scattered energy. It means you are experiencing a sense of focus, alignment, and purpose throughout the whole of your being.

Your energy moving in the same direction is the sense of flow in your work while losing track of time and being fully absorbed in the moment.

Your clear sense of your priorities and values enables you to make decisions and take actions aligned with those core values.

Your energy flowing in the same direction is the calm you feel that keeps you grounded despite the problems and distractions around you.

The feeling of confidence and motivation affirms that you're moving forward on your goals and making progress without getting sidetracked by distractions or doubts.

It is the sense of peace and contentment you feel when you know who you are and are comfortable with yourself.

This holistic energy also means all your spheres of energy within you (body, mind, soul, spirit, and connection with others) are moving in the same direction toward a greater power – how you understand your higher power, be that love, the universe, gratitude, or anything else that leads you toward "GOD."

When all your energy moves in the same direction, this expansive energy provides valuable connections and integration across all aspects of your life. The result is a feeling of calm amid stressful situations.

NOTICING WHAT'S IMPORTANT IN YOUR DAY-TO-DAY

Sometimes, a typical day at work includes several consecutive meetings.

During one of those typical workdays, a few of my colleagues and I had intense back-to-back meetings about a project that was severely behind schedule. On nearly every call, you could feel the intensity and stress of the leadership coming through the virtual communication.

At the third meeting, I said to the team, "Before we jump into the agenda, I want to invite us to pause for 15 seconds of silence. I will be the timekeeper to allow this moment to give us the space to focus on what we need to do at this specific meeting. Are you willing to do that with me?" Team members either nodded yes or gave an emoji thumbs-up. We did the 15-second silent pause and then moved forward with the meeting.

A week later, one of my colleagues who participated in that call and those intense back-to-back meetings said to me, "Denise, thank you so much for that silent meditation exercise before we got into a heated conversation about the project. I felt like I was able to push the reset button within me. It was an energizing moment to help me get through the rest of that meeting."

She said, "That moment of pausing allowed my racing mind to catch up to the present moment. I decided to try that again, and I practiced that silent pause several times this past week, and it worked! It was like an energy booster of focus."

Her feedback affirmed how mindfulness can help you recharge your overall well-being.

How do you notice what's important in your day-to-day?

Living an integrated, meaningful life means you are so focused on the present that you feel aware, engaged, and connected with everything happening at the moment.

This intentional awareness and connection with the present is known as mindfulness.

MAKING SENSE OF MINDFULNESS

Mindfulness is an element of spiritual growth, a category of personal development.

It can be a meditation time, when you sit quietly, focusing on your breathing. It can also be an active part of your day when you intentionally engage with life as it happens before you.

Dr. Jon Kabat-Zinn, a professor of medicine and one of the most prominent writers on mindfulness, defines mindfulness in this way:

> *Mindfulness is a way of paying attention, on purpose and non-judgmentally, to what goes on in the present moment in your body, mind, and the world around you.*
>
> —Dr. Jon Kabat-Zinn

Mindfulness is a way of being present without distraction or judgment.

As a way of paying attention, mindfulness is part of the ancient practice of noticing, called contemplation, that monks and nuns practiced for centuries to help minimize distractions and focus on the present moment.

Mindfulness is a purposeful motion of noticing, seeking, and dwelling on the significant meaning in your life. It means you intentionally take your time with the experience happening before you. It also means you are intentional about taking in the whole experience of the moment and being aware of what you notice before you.

At the beginning of this chapter on forming mindful habits, L.R. Knost's quote highlights that life and work are fantastic, sometimes they suck, and then they are breathtakingly wonderful again.

The challenge is to bring mindfulness to all your life and work experiences. By the end of this book, you will have seven tools to help you live an integrated life of well-being at work.

Working through these seven habits will help you gain confidence in practicing mindfulness in the workplace. Here are 12 reasons why.

1. You keep an open mind and **lead with curiosity** rather than judgment.
2. You are more **comfortable with the questions** than with all the answers.
3. You view spiritual growth as learning from and **walking with others as a listening companion.**
4. You **create a trusted space** that generates a sense of belonging, where everyone is respected and included.
5. You contribute to a workplace culture that **celebrates differences and welcomes diversity.**
6. You hold space for others to be vulnerable, **honoring the conversation** with utmost compassion and confidentiality.
7. You focus on **seeking understanding.**
8. You **welcome others' stories** to help widen your perspective.

9. You **lean in and pay close attention** to the significance of the moment with your colleagues.
10. You **embrace all your positive and negative work experiences** as opportunities for insight and growth.
11. You are **not afraid to share your journey** with your trusted colleagues.
12. You are **okay with the unknown** when life shows up as a mystery.

Reflect for a moment: *How would your life look differently if you had this level of mindfulness and clarity in your work and relationships?*

TRY THIS

Habit Practice – Journal Prompts and Journaling

One of the outcomes of a consistent mindfulness practice is the feeling of calm and being grounded in peace, joy, or centeredness.

First, think about a time in your life or at work when you felt most at peace or experienced a feeling of calm or happiness. What were you doing when you experienced this peace? A walk, a phone conversation, or a simple task such as doing laundry?

Journal prompt #1: *Describe one experience where you felt calm and centered at work or home:*
_____
_____
_____
_____
_____.

Next, reflect on when you have felt overwhelmed, distracted, or stressed. What helped you calm down after that experience?

Journal prompt #2: *Describe one experience where you felt overwhelmed or stressed and the moment that helped you find an inner calm again:*

_____
_____
_____
_____
_____.

FORMING MINDFUL HABITS

CHAPTER INSIGHTS

- Mindfulness is an element of spiritual growth, a personal development category.
- It is the practice of being present and fully engaged at the moment without judgment or distraction.
- Mindfulness is the art of paying attention to all of life – the good, the bad, and everything in between.
- When learning to practice mindfulness, it helps to start by understanding what spiritual growth means to you.
- One of the best definitions of spirituality is from Alcoholics Anonymous – all your energy flowing in the same direction toward your higher power – how you name your higher power.
- "Energy flowing in the same direction" is the opposite of scattered energy. It means you are experiencing a sense of focus, alignment, and purpose throughout your being.

Now that you have learned about mindfulness as a simple practice of being present in the moment without judgment let's explore each micro-mindfulness habit.

The remaining chapters examine the seven habits to help you think clearly, act decisively, and recover fast without burnout. You can practice them individually or by combining several of them. They are not meant to be sequential.

By the end of this book, I hope you discover one to two habits that work for you.

Throughout the book, I strongly advocate the philosophy of Alcoholics Anonymous: *Take what you like and leave the rest.*

Let's dive into it.

Chapter 3

Find Your True North

Hiking is one of my favorite activities.

For the past 25 years, I have been fortunate to have a hiking partner, Mary. We have a similar pace, savor solitude, are comfortable with silence, and share a similar intention rooted in mindfulness.

On nearly every hike we do together, at the start of the trailhead, we pause and ask each other, "What do you seek this day?"

We hold this question in silent reflection throughout our hike. Along the trail, we are attentive to our surroundings, breathing in the forest or mountain landscape and taking in the wisdom of nature. At the end of the hike, we share our insights based on our intentions that day.

One of the best tools for hiking is a compass.

True North is the principal point for compass navigation and a helpful metaphor for where you want to go in life and your work. It is the direction that defines what is most essential to you.

Practicing mindfulness is like using a compass, pointing you toward your True North.

Your True North can be your life's purpose, a belief or core value, an intention or direction. Some examples are a life purpose of providing a loving home for your family, a belief in kindness to others, a core value of gratitude, an intention of a positive mindset, a direction of servant leadership in your work, or a focus towards well-being.

The mindfulness habit of practicing your True North is Focusing on the Essential.

Habit #1

Focus on the Essential

What would it mean to spend the only time you ever get in a way that truly feels like you are making it count?

– Oliver Burkeman, 4,000 Weeks

WORKING WITH CLARITY AND FOCUS

Imagine your work environment if you could show up daily, focusing on what is most essential for you.

Have there been times when you are at work thinking about home or at home thinking about work?

And if you are working remotely, have there been times when you have set a dedicated time to work on one thing, and your mind is distracted thinking about something else?

AWARENESS OF YOUR PRIORITIES

During a team-building meeting at the beginning of our company's fiscal year, our team had the opportunity to share how we work in a virtual environment as our best selves.

One of my colleagues shared that she works early mornings and late evenings because she is offline every workday from 4-8 p.m., her dedicated time to be with her young daughter.

She elaborated, "During this time with my daughter, I don't even take a phone call from my mother or sister. I focus only on her and her after-school time, playtime, dinner, and bedtime."

My colleague was clear on what was essential to her, and the team positively responded by honoring her sacred time.

She later said, "I value this time so much with my daughter that I am completely centered on our time together. Everything else can wait for a while. My dedicated time with her also helps me show up better at work. I know I am focused when I am with my daughter and also laser-focused when working. I can bring my best self to work because I know I will also have uninterrupted time with my daughter."

When my colleague is with her daughter, she focuses solely on being a parent. Work and everything else happen at their own essential spaces of time.

What are the top priorities that help you stay laser-focused on work when you're working and centered on your personal time when you're away from work?

What are your must-haves that you will not compromise on, and how does this help you bring your best self to work?

THE POWER OF FOCUSING ON THE ESSENTIAL

Your must-haves are your bottom-line essentials, core life values, virtues, or top priorities.

Focusing on what matters most helps you stay grounded during distracting and stressful work.

The reality is that we cannot entirely focus on what matters most to us 24/7. We are often distracted during the day, sometimes when work is stressful or when we are not at our best, which is okay. The interconnection of mindfulness and well-being fuels your work through distractions.

When you reflect on what is essential for you, go back to the definition of holistic energy in chapter two on forming mindful habits: all your energy moving in the same direction with your higher power, no matter how you name this energy greater than yourself.

This holistic energy means all your spheres of energy

within you (body, mind, soul, spirit, and connection with others) are moving in the same direction toward your greater power (love, the universe, gratitude, or GOD).

Focusing on your essentials is about aligning your most important values with what you believe and how you work and live – all your energy moving holistically together as your whole self.

BENEFITS FROM FOCUSING ON THE ESSENTIALS

One benefit to being grounded in your life priorities is **stress reduction.**

Developing habits on how you focus and where you place your attention will help keep you calm and anchored in your core strengths, no matter how rough the waters may get at work.

Knowing that you are in control of making choices that align with your essential core values can reduce stress in your life. Research shows that spending a few moments focused on your breathing helps reduce stress and generate a calming peace that helps minimize anxiety.

For example, when you are leading a team meeting, begin the time together by spending 30 seconds focused on breathing and being mindful of what is most important for the team to focus on during the meeting. Be the timekeeper and empower the team members to take a moment to focus on the core task at hand.

The second benefit to focusing on your core value is **clarity in decision-making.**

For example, at the beginning of the fiscal year, each team member shares their top three to five priorities that will drive the most impact on their work. One top priority is universally empowering others to be their best selves.

Another value to bring to the workplace is respect for others. You can filter your decision-making through this lens by aligning personal and work priorities to a core belief (respect and empowerment). With each decision, you can reflect on whether this decision or project aligns with the priority of empowering others to bring their best.

When you nurture and align your work and life experiences with what is essential, you gain clarity in making important decisions. You are clear about what you are saying yes to in your choices. Additionally, because you know what you value, you are firm about what you say no to in your decisions.

The third benefit to focusing on the essentials is the **enhanced quality of your work.**

When you focus on what is vital for you in the workplace, you can give your full attention to each task, each meeting, and each conversation you have with your colleagues.

An example is one of the senior program managers on my team at work. One of her core strengths is her keen ability to listen and anticipate the needs of team members during meetings. During a virtual meeting conversation, she will listen and then share a document, spreadsheet, or a link to other resources in the chat that support the current topic of discussion. Her essential awareness has an immediate impact and helps the team to show up well at meetings.

HOW MINDFULNESS CAN HELP YOU IDENTIFY YOUR ESSENTIAL PRIORITY FOR WORK

The endless cycle of busyness and distractions at work can lead to stress and burnout.

Here are four ways mindfulness can help you focus on what is essential in your day so you can work with clarity and purpose. Choose what resonates with you the most.

1. **Start with a mindfulness practice:** Begin your day with a few minutes of focused deep breathing or quiet reflection. This can help you develop a sense of inner calm, making it easier to identify your main priority and stay centered throughout the day.
2. **Clarify your values:** Take some time to reflect on what you most value in life (relationships, health, career, finances, etc.). Identify the most essential value that you want to prioritize for the day.
3. **Set specific goals:** Once you have identified your essential priority, set a deliberate goal to live that priority in your work. This goal could include

completing a task, making progress on a project, or simply taking time to focus intentionally.
4. **Practice mindfulness throughout the day:** Try to stay present in the moment as you go about your day. Avoid getting distracted by emails, social media, or other interruptions, and focus on the task before you. If you are overwhelmed or stressed, take a few moments to pause, take a deep breath, and refocus your attention on your priorities.

Below are three examples of how you might use your essential core values throughout your day.

Essential Priority#1: Positive team interactions.
- **Example:** Having a meaningful conversation with a colleague.

Essential Priority#2: Meaningful work that enhances your career.
- **Example:** Completing a specific task aligned with your long-term career goals.

Essential Priority#3: Showing up to work as your best self.
- **Example:** Taking a break to recharge your mental and physical health.

With these examples in mind, take a moment to reflect – what is your core essential for work today?

TRY THIS

Habit Practice – Journal Prompts and Journaling

Here are three journal prompts to help you crystallize your reflections and name your core essential priorities for work.

First, focus on your core values.

Reflect on the words or phrases that best describe how you name your core life values (such as family, your spouse or partner, career success, friendship, health, well-being, etc.).

Journal prompt #1: *My top core value is:*

_____
_____
_____
_____
_____.

If you are struggling with this exercise, reflect on the following:

1. **Identify what motivates you**: Consider what drives you to do your best work. Is it a desire to help others, curiosity, or a need to innovate and create?
2. **Consider your strengths**: Reflect on your strengths and areas of expertise. What unique skills and abilities do you bring to your work that you can leverage to create value and make a positive impact?
3. **Set clear intentions:** Identify the specific goals and outcomes you want to achieve in your work. What impact do you want to have, and what steps do you need to take to get there?
4. **Practice self-reflection**: Reflect on your thoughts, feelings, and actions throughout the day. Cultivate a non-judgmental awareness of your experience and use this insight to guide your behavior and decision-making.
5. **Focus on the present moment:** Stay focused and be fully present in your work. Avoid getting caught up in distractions or worries about the future or the past.
6. **Embrace challenges:** See them as opportunities for growth and learning and approach them with curiosity and openness.

7. **Foster positive relationships:** Build strong relationships with colleagues, clients, and stakeholders, and foster a sense of trust, respect, and collaboration.
8. **Show empathy:** Cultivate empathy and compassion for others and seek to understand their perspectives and needs.
9. **Live with purpose:** Connect your work to a sense of purpose and meaning and use your job to create positive change in the world.

What example or method inspires you to stay grounded in your one core value no matter how stressful or challenging work becomes?

Next, focus on how you show up at work.

Reflect on the words or phrases that best describe how you value showing up at work (such as respect, integrity, hospitality, inclusion, positivity, etc.).

Journal prompt #2: *I want to show up at work each day grounded in this central value:*

_____

_____

_____

_____

_____.

Finally, focus on the themes or patterns in your work ethic that reflect your essential priorities.
Reflect on your insights from how you show up at work. Do you notice any themes or patterns? Is there a significant word or phrase that comes to mind? Write it down on a sticky note and place it near your workspace to remind you of what is most essential for you now.

Journal prompt #3: *My one word or phrase to describe my essential pattern of work is:*

_____

_____

_____

_____

_____.

FIND YOUR TRUE NORTH – HABIT #1: FOCUS ON THE ESSENTIAL

CHAPTER INSIGHTS

- Focusing on what is essential to you is a grounding experience in your core values.
- This clarity of focus on your priorities helps you align your life and work with your purpose.
- With this clarity and mindfulness of what is essential for you, you can better focus on work when you are at work and be fully present at home.
- To empower your energy at work, focus on what is essential to you, your core value or belief.
- Focusing on what matters most to you helps you stay grounded during distracting and stressful workplace situations and enables you to make clear decisions.
- Practice consistent reflection and alignment through journaling – integration is a journey, not a milestone.

Chapter 4

Clear the Chaos

Several years ago, I took my teenage niece and friends to a local indoor entertainment center to celebrate her birthday.

Inside was an enormous bouncy house with a ball pit of thousands of multicolored balls that you could jump into and play around in. I allowed myself to jump in and have fun amid the chaos of all those colored balls and kid laughter.

I later thought about that ball pit as a metaphor for life.

Sometimes, life is like a child's bouncy house filled with multicolored balls. Each ball represents an activity, a thought, a task, or one of the many distractions coming at and swirling around you.

It's great to have fun in the ball pit of life. Yet, sometimes, work and life can be chaotic and a struggle.

There are so many distractions coming at you in multiple directions. How do you pay attention to the colored ball you need now? How do you clear the chaos of all the colored balls and focus on the most important ones in your day?

The mindfulness habits that help Clear the Chaos in your life are to Set Your Intention and Make the Most of Your Time.

Habit #2

Set Your Intention

What do I want for my life? Why am I not there?
—Thomas Merton

THE DREADED ANGST OF DISTRACTIONS

Have you ever felt distracted by your phone or overwhelmed by juggling so many tasks and deliverables at work that you struggled to maintain quality relationships among co-workers, friends, and family?

Imagine it is Sunday evening, and you are mentally preparing for the workday on Monday. How do you feel? A sense of dread? Or are you energized and looking forward to a week of doing some of your best work?

If you feel distracted, overwhelmed, or experiencing a sense of dread before the beginning of your workweek, you may find it helpful to pause. This pause will help you focus on what you truly desire in your work and life.

There is one free tool, easily accessible inside you, to help you do this focus every day. It is setting your intention.

ADVICE FROM SISTER ROSEMARY

In 1994, I first met with my novice director, Sister Rosemary. She was the sister who was my companion and guide during the process of becoming a nun.

Sister Rosemary had a round face with bright rose-colored cheeks that radiated joy whenever she entered a room. Her full-bodied laugh empowered you to enjoy life to the fullest.

At our first meeting, Sister Rosemary wore plaid shorts and a red t-shirt with "Sacred Heart" on the front. Throughout her life, she had a way of making you feel at ease in a conversation.

During this meeting, we discussed the goals and elements of the novitiate, the period of heightened study and prayer required to become a nun.

I asked Sister Rosemary what the novitiate was like for her when she entered the community more than 30 years ago, what she enjoyed most, and what her biggest struggle was.

We also talked about my goals for this intense time of study, plus my desire and outcome.

I felt overwhelmed and fearful during the conversation, so I told Rosemary, "I have not lived this way of life before. So much of it is new to me. I am unsure where to begin or how best to study and reflect during this time."

She could sense my apprehension about the intensity of the reflection and work ahead of me.

Sister Rosemary said something that completely changed my perspective on living a meaningful life.

She said, "Denise, remember to breathe. The journey is one day at a time. Before you begin your day praying or serving others, spend some time reflecting on what you truly desire for the day."

"Before anything else, reflect and listen within the depths of your being about what you really want this day. Set your intention first, which will guide your actions throughout the day."

Sister Rosemary's wisdom: True intentions fuel your actions in the day.

Being a nun taught me that my heart's desire is the linchpin, the focal point of strength, for holistic energy and well-being.

Sister Rosemary reminded me that the only intentions that matter are those that lead to action. Everything else is wishful thinking or dreaming.

PRACTICING YOUR INTENTION

I took Sister Rosemary's guidance to heart.

Each morning, I meditated on setting my intention, focusing on my heart's desire and what I truly wanted for the day.

I would wake up at 6 a.m. and make a cup of hot tea. Then, I would sit quietly in a rocking chair facing the convent's back window toward the flower garden. I would meditate and set my intention while sipping tea.

For example, an intention to:

- Serve others with loving kindness.
- Listen and act with compassion toward others.
- Be open to the day's gifts, challenges, and insights.

This daily intention-setting ritual was life-changing.

Over time, I noticed patterns of beauty and nuances of wonder during my daily walks that I hadn't seen before. I listened to others with a peaceful calm of presence and understanding. I felt energized by the daily encounters with insight and moments of grace throughout the day.

Listening to my heart's desire and acting upon that intention made me more grateful.

Here are a few recommendations to help you set your intention each day. These are only suggestions. *Take what you like and leave the rest.*

- **If you have never tried setting your intention before**, you may want to try spending 45 seconds to one minute sitting quietly with your eyes closed and focusing on your purpose every day.
- **If you are feeling stressed or overwhelmed with work**, you may try going for a ten-minute walk during lunch and pay attention to the elements of beauty in nature. Be mindful of what you notice and what draws your attention to beauty or wonder.
- **If you are feeling distracted**, schedule a meeting break. Throughout the day, spend a few moments calibrating your mindset and actions by quiet reflection to reset your intention.
- **If you are worried about your working relationships** with team members or colleagues, you may try journaling about what you desire for your work environment and team.
- **If you are ready to work consistently on your intention at work**, you may want to connect with a trusted co-worker on the habit of intention. Holding each other accountable for your choices can help you be more consistent.
- **If you need help connecting your purpose to your everyday work**, you may want to find a mentor. Working with a mentor can help you be more consistent with your intentions.

- **If you feel exhausted or drained at the end of your workday**, you may try writing a list of gratitude – all the experiences of the day for which you are grateful.

THE POWER AND BENEFIT OF INTENTIONS

Setting your intention is one part. Action on that desire is the other.

Think of this relationship of intention and action as both sides of the same hand. Some call this "practicing what you preach," also known as integrity.

If your intention is off, your whole being feels disconnected. When you are focused, you can pay close attention to the signals of grace throughout the day.

Setting your intention doesn't make you perfect – it is a way to help you seek and live a day that matters for a meaningful life.

And then there are days when work can dishearten or encourage you. An intentional mindset is a mental pivot that makes the difference.

Here are four benefits of setting your intention:

1. **Clarity**
   Knowing your intention helps you clear your mind of the distractions within and around you so that you can focus on the present moment.

You show up in the moment, fully attentive to what is happening. Clarity provides certainty about the experience before you, where you can notice more details.

For example, you might set your intention to be open to your team's insights. This would then lead to a behavior such as asking open-ended questions during team meetings: What challenges have you encountered while working on this project? What are your thoughts on improving the communication channel with stakeholders?

2. **Awareness**

    With genuine intention, you notice what is essential in a way you may have previously missed.

    Even if you are not detail-oriented, you can pick up elements of your experience that provide a fresh perspective. Intention helps you notice the layers of life before you. Your heightened awareness enables you to appreciate the moment.

    For example, you might set your intention to be self-reflective after important stakeholder or leadership meetings. This would then lead to taking time after each meeting to reflect on how you paid attention to your actions and responses during the meeting.

    You reflect on your awareness of your body language and nonverbal cues, such as facial expressions and gestures, and how you intended to project an open and engaged demeanor. You spend a few moments reviewing your listening skills, how you consciously and actively listened to others, and how you practiced pausing before responding to others to avoid misunderstandings.

You also reflect on your biases and assumptions that may hinder others' responses. This quick review after each meeting can help you focus on affirming your experience and discovering ways to improve your impact at work.

3. **Showing Up**
Being intentional about how you show up will help you embrace your work with focus and clarity.

For example, when you begin your day, you might set your intention to show up as your best self in your work. This would then lead to confidence, leading with your strengths in performing your job and interacting with colleagues.

4. **Purpose**
Setting your intention will help give you a sense of direction and purpose throughout your day.

For example, you might set your intention to reflect on your purpose while working. This would lead to being mindful of what gives you energy during your workday, what needs nurturing, and where you need to pause to recharge. You could also reflect on the conversations with colleagues and team members that empower or drain you.

Another practice is an evening reflection on how you did during the day and how this experience will influence your intention for tomorrow. One suggestion is to journal your insights, challenges, and surprises from living your intention at work. Writing down your intention can help you align your behavior and actions with your purpose in the workplace.

Documenting your intention (codifying it in some way through writing, audio, or video) can make an impression on the footprints of your work. Over time, you can recognize the patterns of your purpose at work.

CLARITY OF YOUR INTENTION AT WORK

Clarifying your intention can help you pivot and align with your well-being at work.

In my current job, I have several recurring meetings with stakeholders.

In one of those weekly meetings, I was frustrated with the senior engineer overseeing the capabilities update in a compliance tool that accelerates partner reviews.

He is detail-oriented and quick to explain the current status of work. For weeks, I was not getting the right outcome for my executive updates, plus the deliverables were behind schedule.

He is also easy-going, a sports fanatic, and has a fun, boisterous personality. He engages during virtual meetings and contributes to the team's positive energy.

During this meeting, I asked him for his status update, and he said he needed more time. His lack of energy in his tone of voice suggested he was stalling.

I was frustrated and snapped back with a quick response that we were running out of time. We needed information on the progress of the compliance tool to give to executives who would be making decisions on continuing work in this area.

He promised to email the data points three days later by the end of the week.

After the meeting, I took some time to calm myself and reflect on my frustration. I had a choice to either keep voicing and escalating my anger or find another way to achieve a more favorable result. The pressure to get the data sooner weighed heavily on me. We were already way behind schedule.

I kept asking myself, how could I motivate him more constructively to deliver the results?

I went for a quick walk around the grounds of the office campus and began focusing on my intention for a better engagement with him. The fresh air of the outdoors helped clear my thinking.

With each step of my walk, I focused my breathing on my intention, which became a mantra of a positive outcome no matter how good or bad the data on the compliance tool were. I wanted the next meeting to be constructive for both of us and for us to feel good about it.

I said to myself several times, "My intent is a positive outcome for him and all team members involved in this work."

After meditating on my intention, I scheduled another meeting with him the following day. At that meeting, while keeping my purpose in mind, I told him, "The status report is valuable for the upcoming executive review."

I used the metaphor of a football game, saying, "Think of yourself as the football coach. It's the game's final play, and we are at fourth down with inches from the goal line in taking this project to the next level. Time is running out, no timeouts are left, and we need to make the play by providing this update."

He looked at me like he finally got it. I then reviewed the instructions to determine precisely what was needed. The meeting was brief, like a 30-second huddle before the last play.

He kept his promise to deliver and follow through this time.

I got what I needed for my status report from him by early afternoon that day. Clarity of intention helped me achieve the result. The positive outcome was a success.

STEPS TO SETTING YOUR INTENTION

Here are some practical steps to setting your intention.

This exercise can take five to ten minutes or less, depending on your best timing.

Part 1 – Prepare the Space

Prepare your environment to be free of distractions by silencing your digital devices and placing them out of sight. Sit in a place that is most comfortable and relaxing for you. Set a five to ten-minute timer to focus on setting your intention. If this is your first time setting your intention or five to ten minutes feels too long, set your timer for one minute or two to three minutes.

Part 2 – The Intention

Pause and slowly breathe deeply in a regular rhythm for your body. During this time, you want to clear your mind of any distractions to set your intention with clarity of focus. It's OK if your mind wanders – it happens often. When your mind races or distractions happen, recognize the moment and redirect your mindset to your breathing to reset your focus. Release any self-judgment of a racing mind or unfocused attention.

Reflect on your heart's desire and consider what you truly want in this moment or the day. Focus on setting your intention on a single action. Keep the choice simple, straightforward, understandable, and actionable.

When the timer sounds, breathe deeply and pay attention to how you experienced this time throughout your being. What was it like setting your intention for you?

Part 3 – The Action

After you set your intention, document it somehow – write it, sing it, or speak it. If you don't give voice to your choice, it may remain hidden or become lost in the activities and distractions of the day.

Throughout your day, refer to your intention and periodically self-check to see if your actions align with your purpose. Then, reset accordingly.

REFLECTION

Try this exercise the next time you struggle to achieve an outcome at work.

First, pause for a break. Even five to ten minutes will suffice. Take your time and focus on what you desire for the best outcome in your situation.

Close your eyes and reflect on that outcome. Visualize in your mind or repeat a word or phrase to help you focus on what you truly desire. Then, go and work to achieve that outcome.

Whether or not you are successful with the results, spend some time reflecting or journaling on what you learned from that intention and how it helped you grow through that experience.

By taking the time to calibrate your behaviors and actions with your inner desire or purpose in your work, you can improve your focus and results on your desired outcomes throughout the workday.

TRY THIS

Habit Practice – Journal Prompts and Journaling

It takes practice to be deliberate about setting your intention every day.

The monk and writer Thomas Merton's quote inspires these prompts at the beginning of the chapter. Choose the ones that help you strengthen your commitment to a daily practice of setting your intention.

The first question grounds you in your heart's innermost desire for what you truly want. It is about the reason you are here in life and the purpose of your work.

Journal prompt #1: *What do I want for my life and work?*

_____
_____
_____
_____
_____.

The second question directs you to reflect on the obstacles that hold you back. Think about any roadblocks that prevent you from living as your genuine self.

Journal prompt #2: *Why am I not there?*

_____
_____
_____
_____
_____.

The third question challenges you to focus on changes and actionable steps to get you back on track when needed. This will help you align or realign your intentions, behaviors, and actions toward who you are to be in life.

Journal prompt #3: *How and when will I take action to get there (for my career and life's purpose)?*

_____
_____
_____
_____
_____.

The fourth question invites you to focus on how you will change or pivot and live differently. Commit to the actions you need to do right now to remain firm in your life's purpose.

Journal prompt #4: *Now what?*
_____
_____
_____
_____
_____.

CLEAR THE CHAOS – HABIT #2: SET YOUR INTENTION

CHAPTER INSIGHTS

- Setting your intention is a way of living your purpose, including naming what you genuinely want for your life and then aligning your behaviors and actions in the day to your purpose.
- Setting your intention involves both being and doing; it is mindset and action.
- Prepare your intention, name your desire, and take action to connect your purpose with work and life.
- Begin the day with some expression to declare your intent, such as reflecting, journaling, drawing, speaking, singing, or deep breathing.

Habit #3

Make the Most of Your Time

Becoming is better than being.
— Carol S. Dweck

BEING INTENTIONAL ABOUT TIME

In late 2015, I was on medical leave from work, recovering from major surgery.

Toward the end of the recovery time, my manager visited to see how I was doing. She brought tea and pastries from the local coffee shop. We had a fantastic conversation about life, and the topic of work never came up.

During our time together, she asked me, "Denise,

what are your plans for the new year around learning and growth?"

We hadn't talked to or seen each other for weeks. Somehow, she knew my mind would be thinking about this topic. "Funny you ask," I replied, smiling back at her. "I've been reflecting a lot about this, and I've decided to read a book a week for the coming year – 52 nonfiction books, mostly about personal development and business acumen."

She laughed, saying, "I'm not surprised. I'm glad you're back in good health and can tackle the volume of that learning project. I can't wait to see your reading list."

The magnitude of learning happens one book at a time.

Since 2016, I've read one book a week, which is 420+ books and counting as of this writing. Of all the books I've read, the one that's made the most significant impact on me is *Mindset: The New Psychology of Success* by Dr. Carol S. Dweck, Ph.D.

According to Dr. Dweck, an open mindset means a readiness to grow, to challenge yourself, and to keep learning.

In her research, Dr. Dweck did a study with fifth graders. She gave them intriguing puzzles to solve. Initially, all of them loved the puzzles. When she gave the students more challenging puzzles, children with a fixed mindset declined the problem-solving activity. They didn't want to take the challenging puzzles home to practice.

On the other hand, challenging puzzles were the favorites of children with a growth mindset. The more time they spent on the harder puzzles, the more their curiosity and interest increased. With a growth mindset, children had a strong desire to learn more. Dr. Dweck mentioned that one of the children in the study said to her, "Could you write down the names of these puzzles so my mom can buy some more when these run out?"

Your mindset guides a large part of your life.

I learned from Dr. Dweck's book that growth happens on a continuum of your mindset, not on a binary scale. There are moments in life when we lean towards a fixed mindset; at other times, we tend more towards a growth mindset. Dr. Dweck stresses that we all have the potential to change and move toward the growth side of the continuum.

I also learned from reading Dr. Dweck's research that a consistent mindfulness habit can significantly affect three areas: your mindset, finitude, or how you deal with limited time and decision-making. This chapter will explore all three areas to help you foster the habit of making the most of your time.

MINDFULNESS AND MINDSET

Let's do a quick exercise. Which set of bullet points best describes how you approach the world?

Viewpoint A:

- Mindset is static
- You believe qualities are carved in stone
- Your mindset creates a sense of inner urgency to prove yourself over and over
- You believe you must be flawless right away
- You lose interest when things become challenging
- Your mindset is about immediate perfection
- You see mistakes as failure
- You constantly try to prove you are better than others
- You expect everything good to happen automatically
- The framework is to judge and be judged.

Viewpoint B:

- Mindset is developing
- You believe you can cultivate essential qualities through your efforts
- Success is about stretching yourself – doing your best, learning, and improving
- You thrive on the challenge – the bigger the challenge, the more you can stretch and grow
- You are always learning and making progress
- Setbacks are informative and motivating

- You value what you are doing regardless of the outcome
- You see mistakes as an opportunity for learning
- This thinking leads to open discussion and decision-making
- The framework is to learn and help others learn.

Which examples reflect the most about how you operate at work?

Viewpoint A is typical of a fixed mindset. Viewpoint B leans toward a growth mindset.

There is no right or wrong answer. Each person has a fixed and growth mindset continuum. Plus, you bring both perspectives to your work environment.

The point is you have a choice and can change your mindset at any stage in your life and career.

TRANSFORMING FIXED TO GROWTH MINDSET

Dr. Dweck says that "mindsets frame the running account that's taking place in people's heads."

Mindfulness can help you transform your mindset and help you manage the voice talking inside your head from less of a self-critique to more of a positive internal message.

The fixed mindset can generate an internal message of self-criticism, harming your overall growth and well-being. Dr. Dweck recommends changing the inner dialogue from a judging (fixed) mindset to a growth-oriented one.

This transformation from a fixed mindset to a growth mindset involves intentionally changing your beliefs about your abilities, your approach to challenges and obstacles, and your perception of effort and failure.

Here are five mindfulness steps to help you make the shift. It might be helpful to journal your observations and experiences with these mindfulness steps to find patterns within your thoughts, attitudes, and learnings.

1. **Observe and understand the difference between a fixed mindset and a growth mindset without judgment**: Set your intention to notice when you are thinking with more of a fixed mindset and operating from a growth mindset. Do this self-observation without judgment. A fixed mindset is the belief that your abilities, talents, and intelligence are predetermined and fixed. In contrast, a growth mindset is the idea that you can improve and develop these qualities through hard work, perseverance, and dedication.
2. **Practice pausing to recognize your fixed mindset triggers**: Pay attention to the moments when you feel stuck or frustrated. When that happens, pause and identify the thoughts and beliefs holding you back. Common fixed mindset triggers include self-doubt, fear of failure, and the concept that success should come quickly. Pause and become aware of

the experiences that trigger a fixed mindset, again without any harsh criticism of yourself.
3. **Intentionally reframe your beliefs:** Set your intention to reframe any negative thoughts with positive self-affirmations. Challenge your fixed mindset beliefs by reframing them into growth mindset beliefs. For example, instead of thinking, "I'm not good at math," try thinking, "I'm not good at math yet, but with practice, I know I can improve."
4. **Practice present-moment awareness to celebrate growth and progress:** Instead of focusing solely on the end goal, practice being fully present to celebrate your progress and development. Recognize and be present for the small wins and use them as motivation to keep going.
5. **Practice self-compassion:** Mindfulness includes the intention and action of being kind to yourself and recognizing that growth and learning are a journey, not a destination. Be patient with yourself, and don't let setbacks or failures define your self-worth.

MINDSET AND MINDFULNESS IN ACTION

In the 2023 Super Bowl, the American professional football championship game, the Kansas City Chiefs edged the

Philadelphia Eagles in one of the most exciting and well-played football games.

Jalen Hurts was the quarterback for the Philadelphia Eagles, the team that lost the Super Bowl, the biggest game of the year.

During the post-game interview, he gave one of the best summaries of how to transform a fixed mindset to a growth mindset with a mindful intention:

> *You either win or you learn. That's how I feel. Win, lose, or draw, I always reflect on the things that I could've done better, the things we could've done better to try to take that next step. That'll be the same process that goes on now.*
>
> – Jalen Hurts, quarterback, Philadelphia Eagles, after the Super Bowl loss to the Kansas City Chiefs, February 12, 2023

TOASTMASTERS AND INTENTIONAL MINDSET

Toastmasters International is a non-profit educational organization that teaches public speaking, communication, and leadership skills. Club members meet weekly to practice giving speeches or leading a meeting and receive feedback, all within a safe learning environment.

There are several Toastmasters groups at Microsoft. In the Toastmasters club meeting I participated in, a colleague shared a checklist she wrote for herself based on her research on growth mindset in the workplace. Her words summarize how she intentionally sets her mindset at work.

During her presentation, she said:

"I love my job and am committed to this learning growth mindset where I:

- Stretch myself, take risks, and learn.
- Welcome challenges!
- Choose opportunities that help me grow.
- Accept when I fail – and I'll try harder next time.
- Embrace challenges, and I persist in the face of setbacks.
- Believe and understand that growing and learning requires effort; I'm willing to put in the effort.
- Embrace the opportunity to grow and learn.
- Listen to criticism on how I can improve (instead of shutting down or becoming defensive).
- Find lessons and inspiration in other people's success.
- Reach ever-higher levels of achievement."

MINDFULNESS AND FINITUDE

For several years of my career, I have practiced a closing ritual at the end of my work week.

A ritual is a practice of connecting reflection with action as opposed to a routine of performing the same action over and over again.

When I am ready to end my work week, I open my calendar and pause before I review the following week or month ahead.

I quietly reflect on what I want and need to do and how I want to be and show up for my colleagues, family, and friends.

During this reflection, I tell myself these mantras, "Your time is limited. Make your time count. Make your moments matter." Then, I start filling out my calendar and intentionally blocking out the entire week with meetings, work tasks, and time for reflection.

These inner mantras remind me that my time is limited. I want to make the most of my time, so I include blocks of dedicated time to reflect and do the deep work of thinking and creating.

The time-blocking ritual helps me get the work done to excel in my job and prioritize the inner and creative work to do what matters most.

When you think about a growth mindset, you often imagine expanding the possibilities to help you learn and grow.

The reality is that you cannot learn it all or do it all in life. You can only do so much in 24 hours or 1,440 minutes.

Chronological time is limited to a certain amount per day. It is finite.

No one has unique superpowers where you can bend the arc of chronological time. No person can extend the day to four extra hours when everyone else has 24 hours. Everyone has the same amount of time in the day. Plus, we have limited time in life. We have an end time. One day, our work and our life will come to an end. How do you make the best of your fixed time at work and in your career?

Here are three examples of how mindfulness can help you make the most of your time:

1. **Be Intentional About Creating Valuable Collaboration**: Set your intention to commit to working with your colleagues in a collaborative environment that fosters integrity, transparency, inclusion, welcome, and respect. By bringing this mindful intention to your work, the job becomes meaningful when you work from the strength of your core values.

2. **Set Your Intention to Minimize Distractions**: Another mindfulness practice is to set your intention to minimize distractions like social media and other unproductive activities that can eat up a significant amount of your time at work. To reduce distractions, try setting specific times to check emails and social media and turn off notifications and reminders.

3. **Be Intentional About Taking Breaks:** Regular breaks are crucial to maintaining focus throughout the day and helping you refresh your mind, reduce

stress, and prevent burnout. Use your breaks with the mindful intention to engage in activities that help you recharge, like taking a walk or reading a book.

MINDFULNESS AND DECISION-MAKING

A growth mindset generates a wide range of options and opportunities. The challenge is to funnel those possibilities into the finite limits of time.

You cannot choose every opportunity in your career. Every choice you make in your job is a yes to one option and a no to other possibilities.

Making reflective, intentional decisions can help you carve a path toward meaning. This mindful decision-making is known as discernment.

Discernment is a mindfulness practice of internal listening with your mind and heart and being without judgment or distraction. Funneling your decision-making through careful thought and reflection helps you focus on the most valuable work you do best.

Here are three examples of how discernment can help you focus on your most valuable work.

1. **Inward Listening to Reduce Distractions**: By practicing discernment, you can learn to filter out distractions and stay focused on the task at hand. This can help you avoid wasting time on unim-

portant tasks or getting sidetracked by unrelated projects.
2. **Intentional Listening to Improve Decisions**: Discernment, which involves taking the time to consider all relevant information and perspectives, can help you make thoughtful, informed decisions. This intentional decision can also help you avoid overextending yourself and prevent burnout.
3. **Internal Listening to Foster Creativity:** Limiting your decision-making and focusing on the most valuable work can free up mental space and foster creativity. This added mental space could allow you to explore new ideas and approaches to your work.

Accept that saying *yes* to one or a few options in your career means saying *no* to many other opportunities. Decide with thoughtful intention so you can pivot throughout your career in ways that allow you to show up as your best self and with your best skills.

DECISION-MAKING AS A NUN

Sister Barbara was one of the nuns I met in graduate school.

She was a mentor at the theological center I attended and a member of the religious order of sisters, where I later became a nun.

During my theological studies, we occasionally had

lunch together in the convent kitchen – tomato soup and a grilled cheese sandwich.

Sister Barbara had the eyes of intense listening and had a way of asking insightful, empowering questions. Both the lunches and the conversations were nourishing.

After graduate school, I entered religious life to begin the process of becoming a nun, and my first ministry assignment was teaching eighth-grade religion.

I quickly learned that classroom teaching was not my strong suit. One hundred eighty days of teaching became a grueling endurance test.

I disliked teaching but didn't want to give up or request a ministry change. I joined an order of nuns who were educators and wanted to be my best self in the community.

Sister Barbara was visiting at the midpoint of the school year. I returned the favor by inviting her to lunch for tomato soup, grilled cheese sandwiches, and a conversation.

It was wonderful to see her, and during our conversation, I shared with her how I was not too fond of teaching, including the drain it had on me. In one sentence, Sister Barbara shared some profound advice that would be life-changing for me later.

She said, "It sounds like your energy is in one place while your heart is someplace else."

She was right. All my energy was focused on getting through the school year as a teacher. Yet my heart was everywhere else but teaching, especially eighth-grade religion.

She also said, "It is okay to decide differently in your work."

Even with that, I did not act on the insight, nor did I request a ministry change to do some service with the religious community other than teaching. Instead, I slogged through the school year. I was mentally exhausted when the teaching year was over.

Reflecting on that ministry experience and Sister Barbara's insight, I realized that the challenging teaching experience was an opportunity to pivot and align with work that was compatible with my strengths.

I missed that opportunity, then. I know how to do something different today.

The lesson here is to reflect often on why and what you are doing in your work and be willing to make decisions and changes that generate a thriving career for you as much as possible.

CAREER DECISION-MAKING

Fast-forward to work at Microsoft.

I have been friends with one of my work colleagues since I started at the company. Nearly every quarter, we meet to discuss how we are doing in our careers.

I remember sharing with her that I was looking at a job application for a research position on our company career site. I love to do research, but it was also outside my current work experience as a risk and compliance manager. One of the requirements on the application was ten years of research experience, which I didn't have then.

She saw my excitement and passion about the job description and asked me if I had applied.

I told her no because I lacked ten years of experience. Her eyes widened, and she exclaimed, "What? Even if you don't have the experience and you really want to do this type of work, go for it and apply. Even if you don't get called for an interview, schedule a one-on-one with the hiring manager later and ask them what it would take to work in a similar position in the future."

We continued our conversation about our careers, and then she said something that stayed with me regarding the importance of thoughtful decision-making. She told me, "Denise, what I see in your work is that you are strong as a compliance and risk manager. Maybe saying no to considering the research position allows you to make more decisions focusing on building your strengths in what you do best for the company."

The lesson is to keep seeking possibilities and opportunities with a growth mindset and to prioritize following where your heart leads instead of relying solely on your energy. In addition, reflect and dig deep into why you say yes to one thing and no to something else.

FOR REFLECTION

Reflect on how you are making the most of your time in your work and life.

What helps you be intentional about your mindset, fully present in the moment before you, and make purposeful decisions that foster valuable work?

How are you making the most of your time?

TRY THIS

Habit Practice – Journal Prompts and Journaling

Here are five journal prompts to help you drive clarity and focus on your work.
You can journal at the end of each workday or the end or beginning of your workweek.
Choose the prompts that help you provide the most insights and self-reflection for your well-being.

Journal prompt #1: *I supported, inspired, or helped my colleagues succeed by these actions or attitudes:*

_____
_____
_____
_____
_____.

Journal prompt #2: *The opportunity I missed to help others at work was this, and here is what I learned:*

_____
_____
_____
_____
_____.

Journal prompt #3: *The experience that moved me to empathy with my colleagues at work was this, and here are the insights I learned:*

_____
_____
_____
_____
_____.

Journal prompt #4: *The insight or lesson learned that will help me improve in attention and action is this:*

_____
_____
_____
_____
_____.

Journal prompt #5: *The five things I am grateful for at work today are:*

_____
_____
_____
_____
_____.

CLEAR THE CHAOS – HABIT #3: MAKE THE MOST OF YOUR TIME

CHAPTER INSIGHTS

- Fixed and growth mindsets are two types of thinking we have within us. A growth mindset is about stretching yourself, learning, and improving. A fixed mindset is about proving yourself and expecting immediate results.
- Your mindset frames the mental script that runs through your head.
- You have a choice of which mindset to strengthen, and you can change your mindset at any stage in your life and career.
- Nurturing your personal growth is about leveraging the positive qualities of both a growth and fixed mindset.
- When you think about a growth mindset, consider the expanding possibilities that can help you learn and grow.
- All the possibilities of learning and growth funnel through the finite limits of time and what you can do in a day and your lifetime.
- A consistent mindfulness habit can make a significant difference in your mindset, your finitude or how you deal with limited time, and your decision-making.

- Mindfulness can help you make thoughtful decisions throughout your career (you can't do everything) so you can focus on the valuable work you do best – heart with energy.

Chapter 5

Mind the Moment

Stress happens even for nuns.

As a nun, I sometimes felt the stress and anxiety of managing ministry (work) and life.

The novitiate is one of the stages of becoming a nun, a time of intense study and prayer. My novice director, Sister Rosemary, could read people really well.

Sister Rosemary used one word to help us novices stop and focus whenever she sensed we were stressed. The word was a signal to slow down, pay attention, and notice what was happening before you – one word to signal a quick reset.

She would often say, "Breathe." It was a code word to pause, take a deep breath, and focus on your purpose, on why you were doing what you were doing.

Whenever I did this, I noticed that the stress I felt minimized, and life came into perspective again.

I still use that code word today as a reminder to pay attention to the present moment, be fully engaged, and be focused, especially in doing and being with others.

The mindfulness habit that helps you Mind the Moment is to Practice the Pause.

Habit #4

Practice the Pause

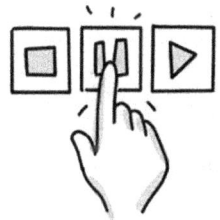

We all need to get the balance right between action and reflection. With so many distractions, it is easy to forget to pause and take stock.

—Queen Elizabeth II

THE WEIGHT OF STRESS

The stress of work felt heavy on a Monday morning.

My first meeting of the day was facilitating a virtual senior leadership meeting on governance. When the team members joined the call, I sensed they were also stressed. They were not their easy-going, relaxed selves. The greetings on the call sounded blunt and felt flat.

Instead of reviewing the agenda, I started with a mindful breathing exercise. I told them, "Hey, before we jump into our agenda and discussion this morning, I want to do a quick one-minute focus exercise."

I quickly found and shared Erin Klassen's one-minute Triangle breathing exercise on YouTube. I told the team, "Focus on your breathing for the next 60 seconds. Inhale when the triangle expands to the shape of an octagon, and exhale when the octagon collapses to the form of a triangle. Let's do this for 60 seconds."

I started the video, and we did the exercise. Afterward, one of the senior leaders unmuted his microphone and said, "Wow, that exercise was super helpful. I have a little more clarity starting this meeting. Thank you."

WHAT DOES IT MEAN TO PRACTICE THE PAUSE

The pause can be a valuable tool for practicing consistent mindfulness.

The pause, a deliberate interruption from your usual routine, helps you reset your focus in the present moment. It can also help you re-settle the experience before you or keep you grounded in your inner strength.

For example, pausing to focus on your breath can help you get through the workday. It is a repeatable process that does wonders for stress management and helps re-ground your perspective.

An intentional break at work doesn't have to be an

extended period. Taking several minutes to pause, breathe deeply, journal, or go for a short walk outside your routine does wonders for slowing down your racing mind and refreshing your mindset.

Here is an example of how I practiced the pause during a stressful work week. At the time, I was feeling overwhelmed by the tasks and projects pressing down on me.

After a morning of back-to-back meetings, I took a break and walked around the building to clear my head. During the short walk, I breathed the fresh air, noticed the buds on the trees, and heard creek water running between two condos across the street.

The outdoor moment was just the break I needed to help reduce the overwhelming feelings of the workload, refocus my energy, and align my projects and tasks with a realistic perspective.

THE VALUE OF PAUSING FOR REFLECTION

The pause can be a valuable tool for consistent mindfulness, especially in the workplace.

It allows you to step back from the busyness, demands, and distractions to observe your thoughts, feelings, and actions non-judgmentally.

While at work:

- Sometimes, you need to step away from your work and give your mind a chance to rest and recharge.

This reset can help you reduce stress levels and prevent burnout.
- At times, you need to clear your mind to return to your work with increased focus and concentration. Reflecting on your work can help you prioritize tasks and make strategic decisions.
- Maybe you need to generate new ideas and insights. By stepping away from your work and reflecting on your experiences, you can see things from a new perspective, create solutions, or accelerate problem-solving.
- Sometimes, you need to become more aware of your thoughts, emotions, and behaviors. By pausing to reflect on your experiences, you can identify patterns and triggers that may impact your work and personal life.

BENEFITS OF PRACTICING THE PAUSE

Pausing for reflection throughout your work can be beneficial for you in five ways:

1. **Improving decision-making**: Reflecting on past experiences and decisions can help you make more informed and thoughtful choices in the future.
2. **Enhancing self-awareness**: Reflecting on your thoughts, feelings, and actions can help you better understand yourself and your motivations.

3. **Promoting personal growth**: Reflecting on your experiences can help you identify areas for personal growth and development.
4. **Improving relationships**: Reflecting on your interactions with others can help you understand how you come across to others and identify ways to improve your relationships.
5. **Reducing stress and promoting well-being**: Taking time to pause and reflect can help you gain perspective on your life and reduce stress.

HOW TO PRACTICE THE PAUSE

Arianna Huffington learned a hard lesson on self-care after collapsing from burnout in 2007.

Huffington is the co-founder of The Huffington Post, CEO of Thrive Global, and author of over 15 books.

The collapse was a defining moment for her, and since that time, she has dedicated her life's work to helping people build healthy habits through microsteps that help them navigate life with less stress and more resilience.

Huffington calls these microsteps "small, incremental, science-backed actions we can take that will have immediate and long-lasting benefits to the way we live our lives." One of the microsteps is a 60-second rule, where she encourages you to spend one minute on a "brief self-care activity that will help you be healthier, happier, more relaxed, or more mindful."

One of the best 60-second micro-practices is intentionally practicing the pause in three steps: stop, focus on your breathing, and listen.

Stop and turn off or step away from your electronic devices. Sit quietly in a chair, take a few deep breaths, and listen quietly with all your senses. This simple exercise, which you can do in a few minutes almost anywhere, is a great way to help you slow down your racing mind and focus on one task in front of you.

EXAMPLES OF PRACTICING THE PAUSE AT WORK

The mindful practice of the pause is to find a consistent time and place that works for you and make it a habit to reflect on your actions, thoughts, and emotions. This can help you better understand yourself and the people you work with and can help you improve as a colleague and team player.

Here are five examples of how you can practice the pause throughout your work:

1. **After a meeting or presentation**: Take a few minutes after a meeting or presentation to pause and reflect on how it went, what worked well, what could have been improved, and what feedback you received.

2. **Before making an important decision**: Take some time to pause and reflect on the potential consequences, alternatives, and what matters the most.
3. **At the end of the day**: Before leaving work, spend a few minutes reflecting on what you accomplished, what you could have done differently, and what you need to complete tomorrow.
4. **After a problematic interaction with a colleague:** Pause and reflect on the exchange, what was said, and how you felt. Think about how you could handle similar situations in the future.
5. **Before starting a new project**: Take some time to reflect on the goals of the project, the resources you have available, and any potential challenges.

TRY THIS
Habit Practice – Journal Prompts and Journaling

The mindful practice of the pause and reflection cadence allows you the time you need to reflect on your insights from your workday.

Pausing to focus and reflect can help you manage your day. Taking intentional time to be still and listen inwardly is a repeatable process that does wonders for stress management and re-grounds your perspective.

Journal prompt #1: *The one insight I am learning about myself from my experience at work today is this:*
_____
_____
_____
_____
_____.

MIND THE MOMENT – HABIT #4: PRACTICE THE PAUSE

CHAPTER INSIGHTS

- The pause can be a valuable tool for practicing consistent mindfulness.
- The pause and reflection cadence allows you to observe your thoughts, feelings, and actions non-judgmentally, free from busyness, demands, and distractions.
- By giving yourself space to pause, breathe, and listen to your body, you can reconnect with yourself and find a sense of balance and grounding.
- The pause can help you combat feelings of burnout and exhaustion.
- Practicing the pause can help you slow down a racing mind to focus on the task, allowing for increased clarity and productivity.
- One-minute mindfulness breathing exercises are some of the best ways to practice the pause.

Chapter 6

Listen to Frogs Before Eating Them

Swallow a toad in the morning if you want to encounter nothing more disgusting the rest of the day.

—NICOLAS CHAMFORT (1741-1794)

A common metaphor for time management and productivity is *Eat the Frog*.

The tip is to eat the frog, the biggest, ugliest task of the day, and do that immediately. Get that done first to be more productive. Brian Tracy's book *Eat That Frog* best highlights this practice.

Another story uses the metaphor of frogs for personal growth.

It is about listening to frogs each day – something I highly recommend before eating them.

A Parable of the Song of the Frogs

An abbess at a monastery in a far-off distant land would arise early each morning and walk down the road to a nearby pond. She would sit by the pond for quite a long time before returning to the convent to perform her daily rituals of monastic life. She did this every day for all the years of her life.

While the abbess was on her deathbed surrounded by her community of sisters, one of the nuns asked her why she went to the pond every day. "Did you go to obtain some deep insights or profound teachings of wisdom?"

"No," said the abbess. "I went to the pond every day to listen and learn the song of the frogs. It is a sacred song that takes a long time to learn."

An adaptation from the article "Learning the Song of the Frogs: The Arts and Theology" by Rev. Edward Foley, Capuchin

The metaphor of frogs is more than just getting things done. It's about bringing your whole self to work and life – starting with your mindset and intention.

The *Parable of Listening to the Song of the Frogs* means to:

- Pay attention and be present without judgment.
- Take time to ground yourself with your purpose for the day.
- Be in an optimal frame of mind to tackle your most important tasks.
- Become centered with quietness and stillness to the sound of life before you.
- Keep listening – it takes a long time, a lifetime, to grow toward wholeness.

Listen, then eat. Pay attention, then act. Listen to the frogs before eating them (metaphorically, of course).

The mindfulness habit that helps you Listen to Frogs Before Eating Them is to Give Grace.

Habit #5

Give Grace

Vulnerability is not winning or losing; it has the courage to show up and be seen when we have no control over the outcome. Vulnerability is not weakness; it's our greatest measure of courage.

—Brené Brown, Rising Strong as a Spiritual Practice

THE MANAGER WHO GAVE GRACE

The manager who hired me at Microsoft admitted to me years later that he was biased against religious institutions.

The hiring manager said, "Denise, I almost didn't hire you. When I first looked at your resume, it had 'Church lady' written all over it, and I immediately threw it to the side, where it landed on the floor near the garbage can. I didn't want anything to do with religion."

"Then a voice inside me said, 'You don't like it when others discount you. You have to give this person a chance.' That inner voice kept gnawing at me because I knew what it was like for others not to give me a chance. I sighed and said, 'OK, I will look at her resume again as objectively as possible.'

"I pulled your resume off the floor and looked at your credentials. This time, I said, 'Well, she has some project management experience.'

"I decided to interview you, and afterward, I knew I wanted to hire you."

The interview process was a success. My first manager not only worked through his bias, but he also gave me a chance. He practiced giving grace to himself and others.

I owe my career at Microsoft to my former boss, who challenged himself to have an open mindset and grow beyond his bias.

WHAT IT MEANS TO GIVE GRACE

Giving grace is about accepting imperfections, resetting expectations, and embracing vulnerability.

Giving grace to someone at work generally refers to showing patience, empathy, understanding, and compassion in professional relationships. This can mean giving people space to make mistakes, extending kindness, and avoiding hasty judgment or criticism.

Let's expand a little on each of these aspects of giving grace:

- **Understanding:** Giving grace often involves understanding the individual's circumstances that may contribute to their actions or performance at work. If a usually productive employee is suddenly underperforming, giving grace may include seeking to understand what's going on in their life outside of work before jumping to conclusions or taking punitive action.
- **Patience:** Patience with colleagues, especially when learning something new or struggling with a task, is essential to giving grace. It allows people the space and time to grow, which in turn helps to create a more supportive work environment.
- **Forgiveness:** Everyone makes mistakes. When a coworker errs, giving grace can mean forgiving them rather than holding a grudge or seeking retribution. This doesn't mean you have to ignore the mistake entirely; it's still important to address it and figure out how to avoid similar issues in the future. The focus is on learning and moving forward rather than blaming.
- **Empathy:** It involves putting yourself in another person's shoes and trying to understand their per-

spective and feelings. Empathy can guide your interactions and help you approach your coworkers respectfully, even when dealing with disagreements or conflicts.
- **Compassion:** This can mean offering support or assistance when someone is struggling rather than ignoring or criticizing their difficulties. Showing compassion helps to build stronger, more supportive relationships with your coworkers.
- **Respect:** Treating others with dignity and respect, regardless of their role in the organization or performance, is fundamental to giving grace. This can mean listening to others' ideas, acknowledging their contributions, and valuing their individuality.

By giving grace, you help create a work environment conducive to collaboration, creativity, and productivity. Everyone benefits when coworkers treat each other with kindness and understanding.

It's also worth noting that giving grace is not about being a pushover or ignoring poor performance or bad behavior. Instead, it's about treating others with empathy and respect and striving to understand and address issues in a constructive manner.

Back to the story at the beginning of this chapter of the manager who hired me at Microsoft.

This manager also gave grace in two ways.

First, he gave grace to himself by understanding his bias against religion and not allowing that bias to have the final say in his decision to review my resume. He showed self-respect and self-compassion by listening to his inner voice, which challenged him to give someone a chance.

Second, he showed empathy and respect for me as a potential hire. He placed himself in my shoes as someone seeking employment, even though he first judged me as a "Church lady" after reading my resume. He reviewed my resume again with an open mind and respect for my experience, even though it wasn't the typical venue for project management.

Remember, giving grace is about accepting imperfections, resetting expectations, and embracing vulnerability.

FOR REFLECTION

Reflect briefly on the following scenario and ask yourself if this has ever happened to you in the workplace.

Scenario: You expect colleagues to behave in a certain way, such as completing deliverables on time or providing thorough and complete status reports. Then, you get frustrated when that doesn't happen. Sound familiar?

Giving grace is allowing the space to give others the benefit of the doubt and trust that they are doing their best.

THE POWER OF GIVING GRACE

What would happen if you trust that colleagues are doing the best they can instead of judging, critiquing, or questioning how they work?

Or what would happen when you start a meeting with the inner expectation of honoring everyone at the meeting and respecting how they show up in their work?

Giving others the benefit of the doubt means giving them the space to be themselves without the baggage of expectations or perfection.

Here are five examples of the power of giving grace at work:

1. **Foster positive relationships:** Giving grace means extending kindness and understanding towards others, even when they may have made a mistake or fallen short. This can help build stronger relationships in the workplace and create a supportive environment.
2. **Improve communication:** When individuals feel they are being treated with grace, they are more likely to feel comfortable expressing their thoughts and ideas. This can lead to better communication and collaboration among team members.
3. **Encourage growth and development:** Employees who feel they have the space to learn from their mistakes and grow are more likely to take risks

and try new things. This can lead to increased innovation and productivity in the workplace.

4. **Reduce stress and tension:** When team members feel they are being given grace, they are less likely to feel defensive or anxious. This can help reduce overall stress and pressure in the workplace, leading to a more positive and productive work environment.

5. **Create a culture of empathy and compassion:** Giving grace means showing kindness and compassion towards others, even in difficult situations. When this becomes a cultural norm in the workplace, it can create a more supportive and caring work environment that benefits everyone.

AN EXAMPLE OF GIVING GRACE AT WORK

One of the positive experiences that resulted from the pandemic was how workers figured out video conferencing amid remote work.

The transition from work to home life or vice versa wasn't smooth or easy. The lines were blurred while you figured out how to balance work, family, school, kids, and pet care. There were video calls with kids or pets in the room, or there were times when you were not on video because you were not at your best that day. Colleagues seemed to accept and honor where people were with genuine sincerity while coping with and managing the various stages of the pandemic.

My team faced a tight deadline during one virtual meeting before launching a new feature. At the beginning of the meeting, one of the lead program managers shared, "I'm not at my best today; I'm struggling right now dealing with an aging parent who lives quite a long distance from me." Three other colleagues on that call were also dealing with aging parents and the stress of managing care for them remotely.

Because the team was trusting, one team member spoke up, saying, "Let's pause for a moment before we jump into the agenda. It's OK how you are today. What do you need? How can we help?"

We spent a few minutes acknowledging the struggle many of us went through concerning care for parents or family members. After giving grace, the team pivoted to the subject matter of the meeting, and a second team member asked, "Can one or more of us help with some of the tasks or take the lead in driving the deliverables to meet the deadline on time?"

In this meeting, where we had to get the work done, there was also time to give grace, have room to honor team members, and hold the vulnerability of our experience with trust.

The environment you create virtually or physically in an office space with your co-workers that provides a safe place of openness and trust is a way of giving grace.

GIVING GRACE AND VULNERABILITY

Another example of giving grace is practicing vulnerability in the workplace.

Dr. Brené Brown is a research professor at the University of Houston. She is the author of six #1 *New York Times* bestsellers and has spent more than twenty years studying courage, vulnerability, shame, and empathy. Her TED talk on "The Power of Vulnerability" has over 62 million views.

She describes vulnerability as "the most accurate scientific measure of courage."

She says the courage to be vulnerable means "to show up and be seen. To ask for what you need. To talk about how you're feeling. To have the hard conversations."

Vulnerability is the willingness to risk imperfections and act with trust among your colleagues.

Being vulnerable means being willing to risk being wrong and exposing your weaknesses to others and your higher power. It also means trusting that others will embrace you with empathy or compassion.

Vulnerability allows for a connection among team members and gives purpose and meaning to your life.

For example, you are transparent with others when you share that you don't have the answers to solving problems. Or, during setbacks in planning engineering fixes, you work with your colleagues to see the failures as part of figuring out the solution.

Vulnerability also fuels your inner courage to connect with your colleagues in trust and without fear.

When you embrace vulnerability, you take fear along with you. Fear does not paralyze you from taking action and growing through the learning experience.

You can generate positive working relationships and create a network of trusted advisors who are your peer mentors. You can lean on this network for strength and support during times of doubt or struggle or when you are not at your best.

Your trusted companions are supporting you, giving you courage and a safety net to be vulnerable in the workplace.

Being vulnerable in the workplace means you are willing to show up, risk imperfection, and have the courage to lean on your trusted colleagues when needed.

Lastly, one of the most valuable behaviors of giving grace is to assume positive intent, the one assumption worth making.

Assumptions are not the optimal mode for work. Yet, the best assumption is to assume that others' intentions are positive. By considering others are doing their best, you give them grace and the benefit of the doubt.

By assuming positive intent, you meet others by listening to understand rather than a bias toward judgment. This constructive assumption allows for profound inroads toward the connection and compassion of others.

You have no idea about the burdens team members carry in life.

Here's a simple way to give grace to others: Reflect on who may need a word or gesture of kindness today, then do this selfless act of generosity.

A small gesture of grace, such as active listening, offering support, giving constructive feedback, being patient, or assuming positive intent, can enormously impact trust and goodness.

TRY THIS

Habit Practice – Journal Prompts and Journaling

Vulnerability helps you understand that there is strength in the broken places of your being.

Practicing vulnerability is a connection with others that fuels inner courage. With vulnerability, you are willing to:

- Show up engaged and present in the moment.
- Risk imperfection.
- Foster inner courage.

These three elements help you lean into your trusted companions at work for strength and support.

Here are two journal prompts for when you need to focus on the present moment and practice showing grace to your colleagues at work.

Journal prompt #1: *What is the one act of grace I can give to someone today that will help me slow down to focus on the present moment with this person?*

_____
_____
_____
_____
_____.

Journal prompt #2: *The one impact from my act of giving grace to someone at work today was this:*

_____
_____
_____
_____
_____.

LISTEN TO FROGS BEFORE EATING THEM – HABIT #5: GIVE GRACE

CHAPTER INSIGHTS

- Giving grace leads to a deep trust in the work environment.
- The two best examples of giving grace are allowing for vulnerability and assuming positive intent in the workplace.
- Through vulnerability, holding others with gentleness and compassion intensifies your listening skills and strengthens your empathic muscles.
- Assuming positive intent helps level-set expectations.
- Let your intention drive your actions toward giving others the benefit of the doubt.
- Give everyone the benefit of the doubt by assuming people are doing their best.
- Allow your opinions and inclinations to lean toward goodness.
- Lead by example – trusting others are doing their best at work.

Chapter 7

Burn Without Burning Out

As a nun, I heard the following story that speaks to the mindful way of living that is energizing and nourishing to your whole being:

> *Abba Lot went to see Abba Joseph and said: "Abba, as much as I am able, I practice a small rule, a little fasting, some prayer, and meditation, and remain quiet, and as much as possible, I keep my thoughts clean. What else should I do?" Then the old man stood up and stretched out his hands toward heaven, and his fingers became like ten torches of flame. And he said: "Why not be turned into fire?"*
> – A Story from the Desert Fathers and Mothers

There are moments when you feel fully immersed in the present moment without distraction or judgment. You fully engage with the task by pausing and reflecting, setting your intention, and doing mindful breathing or some other mindfulness practice.

Sometimes, you may feel a sense of ease and effortlessness, where your thoughts flow without getting caught up by distractions or external stress. Your experience is like being in a state of flow or "in the zone," as some call it.

This experience of flow in a mindfulness practice generates a lot of physical, emotional, mental, and connective energy. You can work throughout the day without the drain of burnout. You burn with this energetic fuel of presence and flow without burning out, and you rise refreshed and ready for the new day.

The mindfulness habits to practice Burn Without Burning Out are to Carry a Symbol of Meaning and to Exercise Gratitude.

Habit #6

Carry a Symbol of Meaning

The world is mud-luscious and puddle-wonderful.
—E. E. Cummings

TANGIBLE AFFIRMATIONS

Before the hybrid work model, I started a new role in a new office building a few years ago.

During my first week in the new space, I noticed yellow sticky notes with affirmations on one of the mirrors above the sink in the women's restroom. The notes were positive messages for anyone who stepped in front of the mirror.

"Be patient with yourself."
"You got this!"
"You are here because you deserve to be here. No one can bring to the table what you bring."
"You are enough."
"You are STRONG."

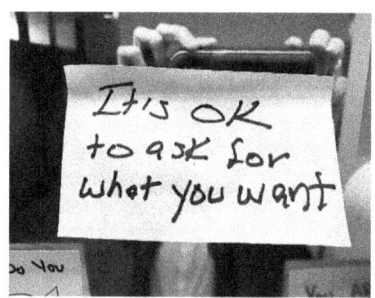

These notes were at eye level, so you could see them while washing your hands or checking yourself in the mirror. They were words of encouragement staring back at you, written by co-workers on my office floor.

At the side of the sink, there was a stack of blank sticky notes and markers for others to use to leave a positive message on the mirror.

The creativity of the affirming messages touched me profoundly.

They made me smile, and I said aloud, "This is really cool." I wrote a few messages to pay it forward on the mirror of affirmations.

The collection grew and enveloped the area of the mirror. They became great conversation starters. Who knew a positive message on a sticky note above a bathroom sink could be an empowering experience?

The messages caused me to reflect on the notes and voices we pay attention to in our work.

Sometimes, the sound of negative or demeaning voices, whether outside or inside of you, can resonate loudly. Some days, these criticisms are all you hear.

The sticky notes on the mirror in the example above are tangible reminders of strength, inspiration, and goodness.

Reflect for a moment on the following:

- *What are you listening to throughout the day?*
- *How can you pay closer attention to supportive messages throughout your workday?*
- *What affirmations reflect a note of goodness for your soul?*
- *In what ways do these encouraging words of power infuse you with energy and determination or bring a smile to your face?*
- *How do you reduce the volume of negative messaging and increase the capacity of the positive and encouraging voices in your daily work?*
- *How do you pay forward that positive message to others?*

THE POWER OF THE TANGIBLE

In 2022, the US market's swag/promotional products industry was $20.6 billion.

In a survey by VistaPrint and OnePoll, 53% of those surveyed love getting promotional products from brands, and 51% say they use them daily.

Businesses spend a significant amount on tokens, totems, coins, quotes, cards, hats, and other trinkets to remind you of something essential or connect with a profound experience.

What is it about tchotchkes, trinkets, and swag that keeps you going back for more?

No matter how much we work and live in a digital world, at our very core, we are still human, seeking connection with the physical, the tangible.

YOUR SENSES – REMINDERS OF GOODNESS

The one tool we all have as human beings is our senses.

Sight, sound, touch, taste, and smell are palpable, tangible tools we embody to relate to one another, our work, and our experience.

At work, do you sometimes long to connect with a significant layer of meaning but need more time to act?

One tangible way to practice mindfulness is to be intentional and focused on what you are doing through your senses. They are the best tools for practicing mindfulness because they are relational connectors.

Reflect momentarily: *Which one or more of your senses helps you connect?*

For example, during one year of remote work, I journaled with The Daily Stoic Journal by Ryan Holiday. I also purchased one of his challenge coins, a symbol to remind you of what is significant for you. On the coin was the Latin phrase from the philosopher Cicero: "Summum Bonum," which means "the highest good." On the other side of the coin is a phrase that reminds you to do the right thing because the rest doesn't matter. This token is something I carry with me to remind me of one of my core values at work.

Summum Bonum Coin in Hand

I work in compliance and risk management at Microsoft. This type of work involves doing the right things right.

When I meet with my colleagues and plan my work, I think about how I can show up, focusing on doing the right thing for the customer and the company. This token is something I carry, a reminder of my purpose for work – doing the highest good.

Sometimes, I will put a sticky note on my monitor with a word of encouragement, gratitude, or motivation to help me be mindful when stressed. It is a tangible practice that helps me connect my core values with my work.

HOW TO PRACTICE MINDFULNESS WITH YOUR SENSES

Here are a few steps on how to practice mindfulness using your senses. Begin by setting your heart and intention. Reflect on what you are seeking at this moment. What is most important for you? (Peace? Gratitude? Calm?)

Know your intention first and then engage with your experience through your senses.

Here are five tangible ways to practice mindfulness at work and home with your senses.

Sight: Spend a few moments gazing upon something beautiful – the ocean, a mountain, a tiny grasshopper on the sidewalk. If you work in an office or a hybrid workspace, take a quick break and walk outside for a few minutes. Notice the natural beauty around you, even if it is a plant or a leaf on the ground.

- What do you recognize? (Wonder? Perspective? Compassion?)
- Be attentive to what speaks to your heart at this moment.

Smell: What is your favorite fragrance that stirs positive memories? You may be unable to practice the sense if you work in a fragrance-free environment. If that is the case, here are some options:

- Go outside and smell the fragrance of nature and your favorite flowers, or breathe deeply the air around you.
- Reflect on what you remember with gratitude.

Taste: What flavors remind you of the sacred, the holy, or your higher power?

- Spend a moment savoring the taste of goodness. It can be your favorite food, a drink, drops of snowflakes, or raindrops.
- What fills your being with joy?

Sound: Listening to music is an engaging way to connect.

- At work, take a five-minute break and listen to your favorite instrumental music.
- Sounds of bells, nature, or laughter can also be a tool for meditation. What rings true for you? Leverage the sounds that help bring you closer to the depths of your soul.

Touch: The tactile connection links you to others and the sacred.

- At work, take a moment to go outside and be within a natural environment. Touch the ground to feel your rootedness in the earth (humility). Hold a delicate flower and ponder the gift of your vulnerability. At home, gently clasp the hand of a loved one and reverence your tenderness.
- What is your experience through touch? (Love? Comfort? Connection?)

ONE MORE TANGIBLE PRACTICE OF MINDFULNESS IN THE WORKPLACE

Here is another way to practice mindfulness at work with your sense of sight and touch.

Curating meaningful quotes or phrases is one tool for mindfulness. It is a tangible way to bring to mind what is important to you, inspire, or remind you of your values.

Some quotes may cause you to stop and think, while others nudge you toward change. There are quotes to stir your heart and emotions. Others can lead you to pay closer attention to your inner life and purpose.

Reflect for a moment: *What quotes nourish your inner being? What wisdom do you need at this time?*

Maybe you need encouragement, comfort, inner courage, or help keeping perspective. Perhaps you seek affirmation or motivation for your work at hand. Having something tangible to see, touch, or experience lets you stay connected to what matters most.

Here's a simple weekly practice for using a collection of quotes as a tool for mindfulness that engages both your senses of touch and sight.

1. Pick five quotes that resonate with you and write each on an index card.
2. Keep the cards with you or anywhere you can access them.
3. For each day of the work week, reflect on one card several times throughout that day.
4. Pay attention to what stirs your soul, plus the insights that come to mind. I suggest writing a few notes on your understanding of the quotes.
5. During the weekend, find five more quotes and repeat the process for the next week.

Save the previous cards and repeat the steps as often as needed. Over time, you will have a collection of quotes for improving mindfulness and soul-tending that you can review and connect with when needed.

HERE ARE FIVE QUOTES TO HELP GET YOU STARTED THIS WEEK:

1. *Be willing to learn new things. Be able to assimilate further information quickly. Be able to get along with and work with other people. – Sally Ride*

2. Don't compromise yourself. You are all you've got. – Janis Joplin
3. Dripping water hollows out stone, not through force but through persistence. – Ovid
4. True wisdom emerges silently, rising up from the Mystery of the unseen Source within all. – Nan Merrill
5. It is good to love many things, for therein lies the true strength, and whosoever loves much performs much, and can accomplish much, and what is done in love is well done. – Vincent van Gogh

TRY THIS

Habit Practice – Journal Prompts and Journaling

This chapter is designed to help you consider how you engage your senses to remind yourself of what is most important to you in your work.

Take a few moments to reflect on the symbols, tokens, messages, or reminders you bring to the work environment to help you focus on the significance of your presence and actions.

Journal prompt #1: *The one symbol I have at work that means the most to me is this:*

_____
_____
_____
_____
_____.

BURN WITHOUT BURNING OUT – HABIT #6: CARRY A SYMBOL OF MEANING

CHAPTER INSIGHTS

- No matter how much we work and live in a digital world, at our very core, we are still human.
- It is human nature to use your senses in work and life.
- One tangible way to practice mindfulness is to be intentional and focused on what you are doing through your senses.
- Allow yourself to carry a symbol of meaning in the workplace that resonates with you and helps keep you grounded on what you most value in work and life.

Habit #7

Exercise Gratitude

When it comes to life, the critical thing is whether you take things for granted or take them with gratitude.

—G.K. CHESTERTON

THE FIRST LESSONS OF GRATITUDE

I learned the practice of gratitude from my parents.

For my parents and family, gratitude is about being grateful for the gift of life and the grace to live this day.

My Dad had one photograph on his nightstand at home.

The 5x7 photo was so significant that he had an 8×10 copy on the wall above his dresser. The image was the USS

Bronstein DE-189, a Naval Destroyer Escort near Iceland in 1945, the ship my Dad served on during World War II.

My Dad is the sailor with headphones on the upper left of the deck in the photo. He is a Gunner's Mate, Third Class, on watch, and is 19 years old. Their mission was to escort plane shipments to aircraft carriers and chase enemy submarines throughout the North Atlantic Sea.

While growing up, I remember feeling cold whenever I saw that photo.

It wasn't until I was a young adult that I asked my Dad about that photo. We were sitting at the kitchen table having a conversation, and the topic of World War II came up. I asked him with sincere curiosity, "What happened on the ship when you were in Iceland during World War II?"

The photo of my Dad (top left) on the USS Bronstein DE-189, a Naval Destroyer Escort near Iceland in 1945.

He took a long drink of iced tea and said with sober intention, "The photo is of me and another sailor on watch. Our ship got caught in an ice storm. We were on patrol in the North Atlantic looking for enemy submarines and became stuck on an ice flow. We were like sitting ducks while waiting for another US ship to respond to our distress signal. We were wedged in for several days and running short on supplies."

My Dad paused, staring long into the distance as if reliving the moment again, and said, "If we hadn't caught any fish, we would have starved. Eventually, another ship reached us to replenish our supplies and help us get off the ice flow. I'm grateful we survived."

His telling of the story moved me to my core.

Although my Dad didn't describe it this way, this photo was a symbol and reminder of his gratitude for the gift and purpose of his life. He lived through that experience, and his life beyond that moment in 1945 expressed his gratitude.

Today, each family member has a copy of the photo of my Dad keeping watch on the USS *Bronstein* in the frigid waters of the North Atlantic Sea near Iceland. It is a reminder to us of the work ethic grounded in gratitude he learned in the Navy that fueled his career:

- **Excellence – Do your best and do a job right the first time.** My Dad was a Gunner's Mate on the USS *Bronstein*. He showed up every day to serve by giving his best.

- **Hard work** – My Dad's experience keeping watch on the icy deck of a ship taught him that your actions make a difference; your results matter.
- **Respect** – My Dad and the USS *Bronstein* crew survived their experience on the ice flow due to their team effort.
- **Gratitude** – Express gratitude in your life, words, and actions. Throughout his life and especially after World War II, gratitude was the bedrock of living for my Dad.

That survival experience in World War II at 19 years old marked my Dad for the rest of his life.

This photo was a daily reminder of his inner strength, resiliency, and determination. It anchored my Dad's mindset that he could get through anything. Most of all, it cemented his spirit in a daily practice of gratitude and appreciation.

PRACTICING GRATITUDE AT WORK

A growing body of evidence in research points to gratitude as the "social glue" for building and nurturing strong relationships. Gratitude can also generate a healthy culture in the workplace.

Science supports practicing gratitude to boost your mood, improve sleep quality, elevate your happiness and a greater sense of purpose, strengthen your relationships, and increase life satisfaction and overall well-being.

Practicing gratitude also gives you perspective on your work and the relationships associated with your work.

Imagine starting every team meeting you lead with one of the following:

- "Thank you all for being here…"
- "I appreciate each of you being here…"
- "I am grateful for this opportunity to take on this project with you all…"
- "We are facing a challenging task ahead of us, and yet, I am grateful to be part of this team working to solve this problem together…"

How would your team meetings improve? Or generate a positive working environment for your colleagues?

Imagine another scenario: you have a small paper notebook and pen on your desk or next to your laptop or computer. Throughout your day, at every hour or after every meeting, you jot down a list or words of gratitude, an insight of learning, or how you listened respectfully to a complex issue with a business partner or customer. Then, at the end of your work day, you open the notebook and reflect on those daily notes, holding them all with gratitude.

How would your attitudes or disposition improve at work?

DENISE PYLES

THE BENEFITS OF PRACTICING GRATITUDE IN THE WORKPLACE

Practicing gratitude is an intentional decision and a choice. Research affirms that there are many benefits to practicing gratitude at work. Practicing gratitude in the ordinary elements of work can have extraordinary benefits. Here are ten of them:

1. **Improved job satisfaction**: Expressing gratitude for what you enjoy about your job can help you feel more positive and motivated. Suggestion: Share positive feedback with your boss or supervisor about a positive experience in your work or with a colleague.
2. **Stronger relationships with colleagues**: Expressing gratitude to your colleagues can help build stronger, more positive relationships. Suggestion: Express appreciation to a coworker during a team meeting.
3. **Increased productivity**: A more positive attitude and improved colleague relationships can lead to increased productivity and better results. Suggestion: Celebrate team successes and milestones with a lunch or a virtual happy hour.
4. **Better stress management**: Expressing gratitude can help put things into perspective and remind you to focus on the positive aspects of your work.

Suggestion: Offer a word of encouragement to a coworker feeling overwhelmed.

5. **Improved mental and physical well-being:** Practicing gratitude has been linked to several positive outcomes for mental and physical health, such as reduced stress, increased feelings of happiness, and even better sleep. Suggestion: Take a moment each day to reflect on something you are grateful for in your work, and make a note or gratitude list in your journal.

6. **Better decision-making:** Practicing gratitude can help increase positive emotions and decrease negative emotions, leading to improved decision-making and problem-solving. Suggestion: Start meetings with a gratitude round, where each person shares something they are grateful for.

7. **Improved customer service:** Expressing gratitude can help build strong relationships, leading to repeat business and positive word-of-mouth. Suggestion: Show patience and understanding and express appreciation to customers, especially those who are challenging to manage.

8. **Increased creativity:** Practicing gratitude can help open the mind to new possibilities and perspectives, leading to increased creativity and innovation. Suggestion: Take time to appreciate the resources and tools you have available to do your job.

9. **Increased employee engagement**: Employees who feel appreciated and valued are more likely to be engaged in their work, leading to increased performance and job satisfaction. Suggestion: Write a thank-you note or email to a coworker or supervisor who has helped you, or acknowledge a coworker's hard work or achievements in a company-wide email, newsletter, or company affirmation/kudos tool.
10. **Building a positive company culture**: Incorporating gratitude and appreciation practices can help create a more positive and supportive work environment for everyone. Suggestion: Get to know the support staff by name and thank them often, such as the cleaning or food service staff.

WAYS TO GENERATE A HABIT OF GRATITUDE

Practicing gratitude on a regular basis is like taking a daily vitamin supplement to boost others and your inner spirit with encouragement and positivity.

There are many activities to help you make the habit of gratitude stick. Here are practices you can easily incorporate throughout your workday or at the beginning or end. Use what is most helpful for you to practice gratitude with consistency.

KEEP A GRATITUDE JOURNAL

A common way to keep a gratitude journal is to list 5-10 things you are grateful for each day or week.

One skill to transform the list of gratitude into a more meaningful note of thanksgiving is to practice the art of seeing. The art of seeing is an intentional awareness of your significant moments throughout the day.

This practice means taking your time to absorb what you notice. It is looking beyond the mundane to see something more compelling.

Keeping a journal helps you become aware of what catches your attention.

Reflect for a moment: What causes you to pause and take a second glance? Who or what stirs your emotions? Then, take mental or handwritten notes throughout the day and bring these intentional impressions to your gratitude journaling.

The gratitude journaling exercise can become more than a list when we note the appreciation with intention and purposeful thought. There is value in making a deliberate note of gratitude. The message can be in a journal, a card, or an outward expression such as art or music.

Being grateful becomes three-dimensional, textured by a savory experience of your day.

HOW TO WRITE A GRATITUDE JOURNAL AT WORK

Here are ten ways to write a gratitude journal at work:

1. Set aside a specific time each day to write in your journal, such as at the beginning or end of the workday.
2. Keep the journal easily accessible, such as on your desk or in your bag.
3. Start each entry by listing things you are grateful for in your work and personal life.
4. Reflect on positive experiences or accomplishments from the day.
5. Write about coworkers or colleagues who have positively impacted your day.
6. Write about what caught your attention in the day that made you pause and reflect.
7. Write about challenges you faced and the positive lessons you learned from them.
8. Write an action of how you will express gratitude for your work and its impact on others.
9. At the end of the day, reflect on your personal growth and learning experiences.
10. Close each entry with a positive affirmation or aspiration for the future.

AN EVENING MEDITATION OF GRATITUDE FOCUSING ON THE WORK OF YOUR HANDS

Your hands provide a unique fingerprint of your life.

Your hands are a tactile way to reflect and express your actions through:

- work
- creativity
- gesturing clarity
- grappling with the unknown
- communicating your purpose.

When was the last time you reflected on how your hands helped you grasp the significance of your being?

Here's an evening gratitude meditation to help you reflect on the importance of the work of your hands throughout the day.

- Find a place to sit quietly with your hands open, face-up in your lap, or hold them before you.
- Spend a few moments examining the front and back of your hands – all the lines, wrinkles, smooth sections, and rough edges.
- See your hands with the eyes of your heart, a heart of compassion.
- Be mindful of the good and positive energy your hands generated today.

- Pay attention to any negative energy your hands may have stirred.
- Spend a few moments reflecting, "For what am I grateful?"
- Speak aloud a word or phrase of gratitude, then breathe the intention of thanksgiving by blowing your breath across your hands.
- Spend a few more quiet moments with your eyes closed and hands open, welcoming a spirit of grace and blessing in your life.
- Afterwards, spend a few minutes journaling any insights from your reflection time.

TRY THIS
Habit Practice – Journal Prompts and Journaling
As a nun, I learned two ways to prepare my mindset for practicing gratitude.

Show Up

- First, show up with a breath of intention.
  - Focus on the rhythm of your breathing. Allow this cadence to slow you down and calm your being. Let your breath help you center on your intention at this moment.
- Second, show up to be still.
  - Find a quiet moment; it does not have to be lengthy. Three minutes a day is a good starting point.
  - Three minutes is also the time to steep a cup of tea – allow the quiet to steep into your being.

Pay Attention

- Next, pay attention with a focused awareness.
  - Become aware of what you noticed in your work today.

- Pay attention to all your work experiences on this day.
  - Reflect on where you noticed the traces of gratitude.

Here are two journal prompts to help you practice gratitude.

Journal prompt #1: *What is one small thing that happened today at work that I am most grateful for and why?*

_____
_____
_____
_____
_____.

Journal prompt #2: *What is one thing I am looking forward to at work with gratitude and appreciation?*

_____
_____
_____
_____
_____.

BURN WITHOUT BURNING OUT – HABIT #7: EXERCISE GRATITUDE

CHAPTER INSIGHTS

- Science supports practicing gratitude to boost your mood, improve sleep quality, elevate your happiness and a greater sense of purpose, strengthen your relationships, and increase life satisfaction and overall well-being.
- Regularly practicing gratitude is like taking a daily vitamin supplement to boost others and your inner spirit with encouragement and positivity.
- Work is a feast of invitations to pay attention. Be conscious of your treasures, reverence your experiences, and express your appreciation with words and actions.
- Many activities can help you stick to the habit of gratitude. Use what is most helpful for you to practice gratitude consistently.

Wrap Up

Seven Micro-Mindfulness Habits

Here is a helpful summary of this book's micro-mindfulness habits.

Find Your True North

- **What it looks like**: True North can be your purpose, belief, or direction in life – the core value within your being and what is most essential to you. People know who you are when you live from your truth.
- Habit #1 - Focus on the Essential
- **An example in your day**: Your core value may be being kind to others, bringing joy and positivity to the world, believing in the Universe, or being rooted in unconditional love.

Clear the Chaos

- **What it looks like**: Life is like a child's bouncy house filled with colored balls. There are so many distractions, and so much is coming at you every

day. How do you notice and pay attention to what you truly want in the day?
- **Habit # 2 – Set Your Intention**
- **An example in your day**: Mentally clearing the chaos in the morning to set your mindset on what you desire. What is the colored ball you are going to pick up today?
- **Habit # 3 – Make the Most of Your Time**
- **An example in your day**: A growth mindset is being open-minded to all the possibilities in life, and all those options ("colored balls") flow through your finite being. You are limited by time and space. Discern, pay attention, and reflect on what to choose, then decide, such as choosing three things (balls) to focus on.

Mind the Moment

- **What it looks like**: Throughout your day, the goal is to be fully present in the present moment, whether you are doing something or being with others.
- **Habit # 4 – Practice the Pause**
- **An example in your day**: Slowing down to pay attention, pausing to notice what is happening before you, or taking a five-minute break to walk outside to reset and refocus.

Listen to Frogs Before Eating Them

- **What it looks like:** This metaphor comes from a parable of Mother Abbess going to the pond every day to listen to the song of the frogs (before eating them).
- Habit #5 – Give Grace
- **An example in your day:** Be intentional about giving others and yourself the benefit of the doubt, practice self-care, and be compassionate toward others.

Burn Without Burning Out

- **What it looks like:** A way of living that energizes and nourishes your whole being, where you can live and work throughout the day without the drain of burnout. You are refreshed and ready for the new day.
- Habit # 6 – Carry a Symbol of Meaning
- **An example in your day**: This is a touch point to remind you of your values and purpose, such as a coin or token symbolizing your purpose, a tangible reminder to reset or stay focused.
- Habit #7 – Exercise Gratitude
- **An example in your day**: Giving thanks and showing appreciation to others is generative and energizing, as daily affirmations of others and keeping a gratitude journal.

Summary of Chapter Insights

This chapter is a helpful summary of all the insights from each chapter in this book.

Chapter 1 – From Nun to Big Tech Program Manager

- The mindfulness skills I learned as a nun helped me pivot in midlife from a career in church ministry to a successful, award-winning corporate job. I had zero business experience at the beginning.
- Mindfulness is the art of paying attention to all of life to discover threads of meaning in the workplace and your everyday life.
- Research on employee burnout has shown that several weeks of mindfulness practice can help reduce stress, improve focus, and enhance resilience.
- As a nun, I learned seven habits that helped me and continue to help me live a reflective, intentional life, especially in my work.
- These habits are not long hours of meditation but short activities that you can do practically anywhere and anytime within an active and busy work environment.

Chapter 2 – Forming Mindful Habits

- Mindfulness is an element of spiritual growth, a personal development category.
- It is the practice of being present and fully engaged at the moment without judgment or distraction.
- Mindfulness is the art of paying attention to all of life – the good, the bad, and everything in between.
- When learning to practice mindfulness, it helps to start by understanding what spiritual growth means to you.
- One of the best definitions of spirituality is from Alcoholics Anonymous – all your energy flowing in the same direction toward your higher power – how you name your higher power.
- "Energy flowing in the same direction" is the opposite of scattered energy. It means you are experiencing a sense of focus, alignment, and purpose throughout your being.

Chapter 3 – Find Your True North – Habit #1 - Focus on the Essential

- Focusing on what is essential to you is a grounding experience in your core values.
- This clarity of focus on your priorities helps you align your life and work with your purpose.

- With this clarity and mindfulness of what is essential for you, you can better focus on work when you are at work and be fully present at home.
- To empower your energy at work, focus on what is essential to you, your core value or belief.
- Focusing on what matters most to you helps you stay grounded during distracting and stressful workplace situations and enables you to make clear decisions.
- Practice consistent reflection and alignment through journaling – integration is a journey, not a milestone.

Chapter 4 – Clear the Chaos – Habit #2 – Set Your Intention

- Setting your intention is a way of living your purpose, including naming what you genuinely want for your life and then aligning your behaviors and actions in the day to your purpose.
- Setting your intention involves both being and doing; it is mindset and action.
- Prepare your intention, name your desire, and take action to connect your purpose with work and life.
- Begin the day with some expression to declare your intent, such as reflecting, journaling, drawing, speaking, singing, or deep breathing.

Chapter 4 – Clear the Chaos – Habit #3 – Make the Most of Your Time

- Fixed and growth mindsets are two types of thinking we have within us. A growth mindset is about stretching yourself, learning, and improving. A fixed mindset is about proving yourself and expecting immediate results.
- Your mindset frames the mental script that runs through your head.
- You have a choice of which mindset to strengthen, and you can change your mindset at any stage in your life and career.
- Nurturing your personal growth is about leveraging the positive qualities of both a growth and fixed mindset.
- When you think about a growth mindset, consider the expanding possibilities that can help you learn and grow.
- All the possibilities of learning and growth funnel through the finite limits of time and what you can do in a day and your lifetime.
- A consistent mindfulness habit can make a significant difference in your mindset, your finitude, or how you deal with limited time, and your decision-making.
- Mindfulness can help you make thoughtful decisions throughout your career (you can't do every-

thing) so you can focus on the valuable work you do best – heart with energy.

Chapter 5 – Mind the Moment – Habit #4 – Practice the Pause

- The pause can be a valuable tool for practicing consistent mindfulness.
- The pause and reflection cadence allows you to observe your thoughts, feelings, and actions non-judgmentally, free from busyness, demands, and distractions.
- By giving yourself space to pause, breathe, and listen to your body, you can reconnect with yourself and find a sense of balance and grounding.
- The pause can help you combat feelings of burnout and exhaustion.
- Practicing the pause can help you slow down a racing mind to focus on the task, allowing for increased clarity and productivity.
- One-minute mindfulness breathing exercises are some of the best ways to practice the pause.

Chapter 6 – Listen to Frogs Before Eating Them – Habit #5 – Give Grace

- Giving grace leads to a deep trust in the work environment.

- The two best examples of giving grace are allowing for vulnerability and assuming positive intent in the workplace.
- Through vulnerability, holding others with gentleness and compassion intensifies your listening skills and strengthens your empathic muscles.
- Assuming positive intent helps level-set expectations.
- Let your intention drive your actions toward giving others the benefit of the doubt.
- Give everyone the benefit of the doubt by assuming people are doing their best.
- Allow your opinions and inclinations to lean toward goodness.
- Lead by example – trusting others are doing their best at work.

Chapter 7 – Burn Without Burning Out – Habit #6 – Carry a Symbol of Meaning

- No matter how much we work and live in a digital world, at our very core, we are still human.
- It is human nature to use your senses in work and life.
- One tangible way to practice mindfulness is to be intentional and focused on what you are doing through your senses.
- Allow yourself to carry a symbol of meaning in the

workplace that resonates with you and helps keep you grounded on what you most value in work and life.

Chapter 7 – Burn Without Burning Out – Habit #7 – Exercise Gratitude

- Science supports practicing gratitude to boost your mood, improve sleep quality, elevate your happiness and a greater sense of purpose, strengthen your relationships, and increase life satisfaction and overall well-being.
- Regularly practicing gratitude is like taking a daily vitamin supplement to boost others and your inner spirit with encouragement and positivity.
- Work is a feast of invitations to pay attention. Be conscious of your treasures, reverence your experiences, and express your appreciation with words and actions.
- Many activities can help you stick to the habit of gratitude. Use what is most helpful for you to practice gratitude consistently.

Summary of Journal Prompts

You can find all the journal prompts from each book chapter in this section.

Chapter 1 – From Nun to Big Tech Program Manager
Journal prompt: *The one thing that helps me pay attention and be fully present to what is happening at work is this:*

Chapter 2 – Forming Mindful Habits
Journal prompt: *Describe one experience where you felt calm and centered at work or home:*

Journal prompt: *Describe one experience where you felt overwhelmed or stressed and the moment that helped you find an inner calm again:*

Chapter 3 – Find Your True North – Habit #1 – Focus on the Essential
Journal prompt: *My top core value is:*

Journal prompt: *I want to show up at work each day grounded in this central value:*

Journal prompt: *My one word or phrase to describe my essential pattern of work is:*

Chapter 4 – Clear the Chaos – Habit #2 – Set Your Intention
   Journal prompt: *What do I want for my life and work?*
   Journal prompt: *Why am I not there?*
   Journal prompt: *How and when will I take action to get there (for my career and life's purpose)?*
   Journal prompt: *Now what?*

Chapter 4 – Clear the Chaos – Habit #3 – Make the Most of Your Time
   Journal prompt: *I supported, inspired, or helped my colleagues succeed by these actions or attitudes:*
   Journal prompt: *The opportunity I missed to help others at work was this, and here is what I learned:*
   Journal prompt: *The experience that moved me to empathy with my colleagues at work was this, and here are the insights I learned:*
   Journal prompt: *The insight or lesson learned that will help me improve in attention and action is this:*
   Journal prompt: *The five things I am grateful for at work today are*:

Chapter 5 – Mind the Moment – Habit #4 – Practice the Pause
   Journal prompt: *The one insight I am learning about myself from my insights at work today is this:*

Chapter 6 – Listen to Frogs Before Eating Them – Habit #5 – Give Grace

> **Journal prompt:** *What is the one act of grace I can give to someone today that will help me slow down to focus on the present moment with this person?*
>
> **Journal prompt:** *The one impact from my act of giving grace to someone at work today was this:*

Chapter 7 – Burn Without Burning Out – Habit #6 – Carry a Symbol of Meaning

> **Journal prompt:** *The one symbol I have at work that means the most to me is this:*

Chapter 7 – Burn Without Burning Out – Habit #7 – Exercise Gratitude

> **Journal prompt:** *What is one small thing that happened today at work that I am most grateful for and why?*
>
> **Journal prompt:** *What is one thing I am looking forward to at work with gratitude and appreciation?*

Bonus Reflection
10 Essentials For Mindfulness At Work

One of my favorite activities is hiking.

Every time I go into nature, I carry the "ten essentials" with me. These items are vital tools I have in my pack and know how to use whether hiking the backcountry, on a trail in the mountains, or a familiar footpath in a local forest or park.

Their purpose is to help prepare for an emergency in the outdoors or handle a situation if something doesn't go as planned on the trail. The ten essentials are the must-haves for hiking.

Ten Essentials for Hiking

1. Navigation
2. Light: Headlamp or Flashlight
3. Sun Protection
4. First Aid Kit
5. Knife or Hatchet
6. Fire-Starting Capability
7. Shelter, Tent, or Bivy

8. Day's Supply of Extra Food
9. Extra Water or Water Purification System
10. Extra Clothes

What are your must-have essentials at work?

What will help you show up at work as your best self, prepared and ready to handle any situation?

What will help you overcome stressful moments and remain true to your core purpose?

To inspire you, here are a few of mine:

1. **A mindset of intention:** My headlamp for direction at work.
2. **An attitude of welcoming others and giving grace:** The starting capability for building connections and trust among the team.
3. **A notebook and pen:** I use them to take notes, troubleshoot, and discover the wisdom to generate meaningful work with purpose.

10 ESSENTIALS FOR MINDFULNESS AT WORK

Imagine mindfulness is like a compass pointing you toward your true north of what you believe in (be that love, the universe, courage, a higher power, kindness, etc.).

Below is a list of the ten essentials for mindfulness and how they can help you focus on what is most important to you in the workplace.

Think of these essentials as metaphors or symbols to help you sustain your well-being at work during stressful moments or times of uncertainty. They are like a mental checklist for your mindset and well-being.

These are only suggestions. Choose one or two that resonate with you. Use what is helpful to connect with what is most important in how you show up at work, centered on your essential core values.

1. **Navigation**
   - Reflect on the coming year at work and have a plan or a roadmap that aligns your core life values with your career, job, and work.
   - What direction are you headed in your career?
   - How is your inner compass guiding your work with your colleagues?
   - Are your work and personal mission statements, goals, or vision boards in sync? If not, what needs to shift or change direction?
   - Knowing where you are going or what you are doing at a particular time of the day can help you focus your intention and attention on the work at hand.
2. **Hydration**
   - Reflect on what will nourish you during times of stagnation or feeling stuck.
   - Is there a word, key phrase, symbol, or photograph that inspires or sustains your well-being?

- Focus on why and what you are doing at work instead of mindless meandering through your job.
- Hydrate your mindset daily to what is most important to you.

3. **Nutrition**
    - Another source of inner nourishment is to feed your mind with a steady diet of positive thoughts and nourishing energy to keep you strong in your values.
    - Reflect for a moment on anything "eating at you" internally. Are you distracted, bothered, or stressed by something that gets in the way of your best work?
    - Next, reflect on moments when you felt good about focusing on the essential elements of your work. What helped you sustain this clarity?
    - List words, phrases, song lyrics, or quotes affirming the connection between your core values and your work environment.
    - Feed your mindset with positive nourishment.

4. **Rain Gear and Insulation**
    - Reflect on how you protect your core values during times of difficulty at work.
    - Pay attention to what you need to care for yourself amid work challenges or changes.

- How do you insulate yourself from verbal or non-verbal signals distracting you from being laser-focused on doing what truly matters in your work?
- Ensure the protective gear doesn't block you from the difficulty but helps you manage through the growth.

5. **Firestarter**
   - Reflect on who or what your sources of inspiration and action are.
   - Motivational reading? Inner determination? Mentors? Coaches?
   - Have a collection of go-to writings for inspiration to help keep you grounded in your priorities.
   - Know your go-to spark of inspiration when you need the motivation to act from your critical values.

6. **First Aid Kit**
   - Reflect on your readiness and how you will respond when you hit bumps and bruises in the workplace.
   - What is your healing balm?
   - How do you keep perspective, stay courageous, or practice self-care?
   - Foster a mindset and awareness that sees failure and setbacks as part of your career learning process and an opportunity for growth.

7. **Tools**
   - There are a plethora of multitools available to help you grow personally.
   - Reflect on the ones you want to keep with you to help you navigate your career with focused attention.
   - Keep a journal to reflect on your thoughts and experiences. There are many ways to utilize one (analog, digital, audio, video). Over time, these reflections can offer patterns of insight and wisdom in your career.
   - This tool is your go-to mechanism to help you remain centered in your commitment to focused growth, no matter the distractions.
8. **Illumination**
   - Reflect on what is foundational within the core of your being to light your path forward in your work and career. Some examples are the values of integrity, inclusion, empathy, kindness, respect, and gratitude.
   - Know what helps radiate your guiding principle no matter the difficulty, stress, or challenge at work.
9. **Sun Protection**
   - Reflect on what will protect you when things become "too much." Too much distraction, stress, or feeling overwhelmed.

- What will help you endure change, struggle, and growth cycles?
- Lean toward positive self-talk to minimize self-doubt or self-criticism and friends who can listen with empathy and perspective.
- Keep a healthy perspective on protecting the core values that empower you with strength rather than isolate you with weakness.

10. **Shelter**
    - Reflect on who or what helps bring you back to the center of your being. Some examples are a trusted advisor, a team member, a book, a quote, or music lyrics.
    - Know what helps you remain steadfast in your commitment to your core priorities.

Acknowledgments

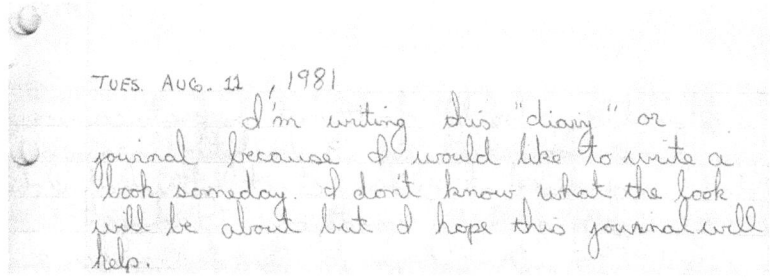

My First Journal Entry, Louisville, KY

I am grateful to my parents, family, friends, and mentors for honoring my writing gifts and encouraging me to keep journaling since that first entry in 1981.

Thank you to Akash Karia for your coaching, listening, and encouragement in bringing out my best writing in this book.

I am most grateful for Nicolas Cole, Dickie Bush, and the Ship 30 Writing Community, who keep empowering me to improve my writing skills.

I appreciate the coaching from Ramon Williamson for helping me land on the micro-mindfulness habits.

Thank you to my beta readers, John Bartol, Peggy Crowley, Nedra Gallagher, Isabelle Hebrant, John Moore, and Bal Simon, for your feedback on the outline and sketchy first draft. I greatly appreciate your valuable commentary.

To Mary, my *anam cara,* confidante, the ISTJ to my ENFP, the first editorial pen to my work, I am grateful for helping me write with clarity, and most of all, for the soulful conversations between the edits.

Finally, thank you, the reader of this book, for taking the time to walk with me on this journey. Here's to living a life of purpose and meaning one moment at a time. *Pax et bonum.*

Notes

Chapter 1 – From Nun to Big Tech Program Manager

At the time of this publication, I work for Microsoft. All opinions in this book are my own. The stories and people are real.

The quote from Satya Nadella, Microsoft's CEO at the time of this publication, is from a small 3x5 notebook journal I received from the company: A Small Book of Big Thought, 2017. The quote is on the last page to inspire employees to make work meaningful.

The photo of the nuns in habit is a stock photo purchased from Getty Images, iStock photo ID 912716394. Two nuns in habit are holding a city map and talking with each other in Rome, Italy, on April 22, 2015. A habit is unique clothing that distinguishes nuns from monks. The habits are usually monochromatic – black, white, or gray.

Research on employee burnout has shown that several weeks of mindfulness practice can help reduce stress, improve focus, and enhance resilience. 4 Ways Mindfulness Traits and Practices Build Resilience | Psychology Today.

The research data on the science of mindfulness also comes from the article "The Science of Mindfulness." By the Mindful Staff of Mindful Magazine, August 31, 2022.

Chapter 2 – Forming Mindful Habits

The quote by L.R. Knost is one of my favorites. L.R. Knost is an award-winning author, feminist, and social justice activist. She is the founder and director of the children's rights advocacy and family consulting group Little Hearts/Gentle Parenting Resources. She is also the Editor-in-Chief of Holistic Parenting Magazine.

Alcoholics Anonymous (AA) is a global organization that aims to help alcoholics achieve sobriety. Membership is open to anyone who wants to do something about their drinking problem.

Dr. Jon Kabat-Zinn, Ph.D., is a Professor of Medicine emeritus at the University of Massachusetts Medical School and founder of the world-renowned Mindfulness-Based Stress Reduction (MBSR) Clinic in 1979. His writing has contributed to the growing movement of mindfulness into mainstream institutions. The quote is from *Jon Kabat Zinn – In His Own Words* by Raymond Wells, 2022. I also highly recommend the book *Full Catastrophe Living (Revised Edition): Using the Wisdom of Your Body and Mind to Face Stress, Pain, and Illness.* 2013.

Chapter 3 – Find Your True North – Habit #1: Focus on the Essential

One of the best resources for compass navigation is the *Mountaineers Books Wilderness Navigation: Finding Your Way Using Map, Compass, Altimeter & GPS – Third Edition.*
    The quote by Oliver Burkeman is from his book *Four Thousand Weeks: Time Management for Mortals.* 2021. p. 205.
    Research shows that even one minute of focused, slow, intentional breathing exercises can impact stress reduction; from the article "This Slow-Breathing Exercise Can Reduce Stress and Anxiety" | Psychology Today

Chapter 4 – Clear the Chaos – Habit #3: Set Your Intention

The quote by Thomas Merton comes from my friend and spiritual mentor, Rev. Tim Clark, a former monk from Our Lady of Guadalupe Trappist Abbey in Carlton, OR, and as of this writing, a diocesan priest of the Archdiocese of Seattle, WA. Thomas Merton (1915-1968) was a monk of the Abbey of Gethsemani in Trappist, KY, and was one of the most influential American Catholic authors of the 20th century. He was also a prolific writer on contemplation (another word for mindfulness). His writing is still relevant today.

Chapter 4 – Clear the Chaos – Habit #3: Make the Most of Your Time

The quote at the beginning of this chapter is from *Mindset: The New Psychology of Success* by Dr. Carol S. Dweck, Ph.D., 2007. p. 25. Her research on puzzle solving with fifth-grade students is on p. 23. The quote on "mindsets frame the running account that's taking place in people's heads" is on p. 215.

Here is the article: "Jalen Hurts shares thoughtful message after Eagles lose Super Bowl 57 to Chiefs: 'You either win or you learn'" on quarterback Jalen Hurts and his message after the Philadelphia Eagles lost to the Kansas City Chiefs. You can hear his quote on the Twitter video embedded in the article.

Toastmasters International is a nonprofit educational organization that teaches public speaking and leadership skills. The organization has a worldwide network of clubs to help members become more confident as speakers, leaders, and communicators. Thank you to my colleague Anne Stein for sharing her insights for this book.

Chapter 5 – Mind the Moment – Habit #4: Practice the Pause

This quote by Queen Elizabeth II at the beginning of this chapter is from Her Majesty's Christmas Broadcast, December 2013.

See Erin Klassen's simple <u>One-Minute Triangle Breathing Exercise on YouTube</u>.

Arianna Huffington is the founder and CEO of <u>Thrive Global</u>, a platform and mission to end the burnout epidemic. See her article "<u>Microsteps: The Big Idea That's Too Small to Fail</u>."

Chapter 6 – Listen to Frogs Before Eating Them – Habit #5: Give Grace

The quote at the beginning of this chapter is credited to Nicolas Chamfort, a French writer during the 1790s and the French Revolution. <u>Quote Investigator</u> has an excellent history of this quote about swallowing a toad in the morning. The words are credited to Mr. de Lassay, who served as a mouthpiece for Chamfort. Also, according to Quote Investigator, there is no substantial evidence that Mark Twain wrote the expression.

<u>Eat That Frog!: 21 Great Ways to Stop Procrastinating and Get More Done in Less Time. Third Edition by Brian Tracy, 2017.</u> This book is a classic on productivity.

I first heard the story of "The Song of the Frogs" from Mr. Gabe Huck, the Director of Liturgy Training Publications, who was the commencement speaker during my graduation from the Catholic Theological Union in June 1993, where I received my Master of Divinity. This is the parable in Huck's words:

Among the many Zen-like, finish-it-yourself stories of the Hasidic rabbis is this one about a conversation among disciples immediately after a great master's death. One of his disciples asked several others: "Do you know why our master went to the pond every day at dawn and stayed there for a little while before coming home again?" They did not know. The one who had asked told them: "He was learning the song with which the frogs praise God. It takes," the disciple added, "it takes a very long time to learn that song."
—Gabe Huck, June 1993.

One of my professors, the Rev. Edward Foley Capuchin, published the story in his article, "Learning the Song of the Frogs: The Arts and Theology," National Association of Pastoral Musicians Pastoral Music Magazine, Vol 18. No. 4, April – May 1994, pp. 28-30, 37-39. *(Out of print.)* The quote in this book is an adaptation of the story.

The chapter references the term "Church Lady," a character created by Dana Carvey and performed on Saturday Night Live.

Rising Strong as a Spiritual Practice by Brené Brown, June 2017: I have listened to this audiobook multiple times. Dr. Brené Brown offers the best data and writing on vulnerability, belonging, and wholehearted living.

Dr. Brené Brown is a researcher, storyteller, and Texan. I highly recommend her TED talk on The Power of Vulnerability.

Chapter 7 – Burn Without Burning Out – Habit #6: Carry a Symbol of Meaning

The story from the Desert Fathers and Mothers at the beginning of the chapter is from the Monasteries of the Heart – Journal Entry 228.

This quote is from Edward Estlin Cummings (1894 – 1962), also known as e.e. cummings, an American poet and author known for his modern free-form poetry.

The photos in this chapter show sticky notes of positive affirmation and encouragement in the women's restroom at one of the office buildings on the Microsoft campus, Redmond, WA.

2022 statistics on the promotional products industry in the US was $20.6 billion.

A survey by VistaPrint and OnePoll came from the article, "Half of Americans Love Getting Promotional Swag from Brands": Poll. September, 2022.

The photo is the token I carry that reminds me of doing the highest good, the Summum Bonum Medallion at the Daily Stoic. It is an expression from the great Roman orator Cicero. The Latin inscription means "the highest good."

The quote is from Sally Ride (1951-2012), the first American woman to fly in space.

The quote is from Janis Joplin (1943-1970), an American blues singer in the 1960s.

The quote from <u>Ovid (43 BCE-17/18 CE)</u> – a Roman poet during the reign of Augustus.

The quote from <u>Nan Merrill (1931-2010)</u>: In 1987, Nan Merrill began an urban contemplative community welcoming individuals of all faiths and cultures called *Friends of Silence*. The community has grown from 40 members to an international community of over 6,000. Friends of Silence is one of my favorite resources for curated quotes on mindfulness, contemplation, and prayer.

The quote is from <u>Vincent van Gogh (1853-1890)</u>, a Dutch artist considered one of the greatest Post-Impressionist painters.

Chapter 7 – Burn Without Burning Out – Habit #7: Exercise Gratitude

The quote at the beginning of the chapter is by <u>G.K. Chesterton (1874-1936)</u> – an English writer and philosopher.

The black-and-white photo in this chapter shows my Dad on watch aboard the USS *Bronstein* DE-189 Naval Destroyer Escort near Iceland in 1945 during World War II.

Research comes from the article "<u>The Science of Gratitude</u>." Mindful Magazine. February 17, 2022.

Bonus Reflection – 10 ESSENTIALS FOR MINDFULNESS AT WORK

Recreational Equipment Incorporated (REI) has a great checklist on the Ten Essentials for hiking and backpacking.

About the Author

Denise Pyles is a writer, speaker, and micro-mindfulness coach.

Her mission is to empower others to find nurturing stillness within a distracted world.

Denise is a former nun with over 35,000 hours of mindfulness practice. She brings a unique background that combines deep mindfulness expertise with an understanding of the challenges faced in the tech sector.

She writes about three topics of micro-mindfulness to help you find meaning in your everyday work and life: one-sentence journaling, practicing the intentional pause, and mindful self-talk mantras.

Denise lives in Edmonds, Washington, and enjoys hiking the outdoors. She practices mindfulness with a camera, notebook, pen, and backpack full of curiosity.

Want to Learn More?

HOW I CAN HELP YOU

Are you sometimes easily distracted by your thoughts or all the digital shiny objects? If so, you might want to try my course on learning micro-mindfulness practices to help you increase resilience at startmicromindfulness.com.

Are you gaining some traction in practicing mindfulness? Want to take it to the next level of consistency? Consider my 14-day one-sentence consistent mindfulness journaling challenge at 1sentencejournaling.com.

Do you struggle to make time in your busy schedule to practice mindfulness? Would you like to receive easy micro-mindfulness tips every Sunday on practicing mindfulness without feeling like it's one more thing on your calendar? Join Daring Perspectives on Micro-Mindfulness Practices.

For more free resources on practicing micro-mindfulness, visit denisepyles.com.